"This is not an 'easy' book. It is a genuine original. (And I know how overused that word is.) It will—should—must change your life. I know Tim Sanders—and he and this book are for real. Believe it. And become a (wildly successful) 'lovecat.'"

—**TOM PETERS**, author of the bestselling
In Search of Excellence and *Reinventing Work Series*

"Sanders's brand of 'biz-love' is grounded in solid, practical steps." —*Christian Science Monitor*

"Tim Sanders is one of the most creative, articulate, and thought-provoking executives I have met. Our clients rave about Tim and his fresh approach to business. You will be energized and inspired after reading *Love Is the Killer App*."

—**JEFF RICH**, president and CEO of
Affiliated Computer Services, Inc.

"Tim Sanders is not your ordinary business guy, and this is not your ordinary business book. Sanders evangelizes on the value of shared knowledge, the power of personal networks, and the karma of human compassion. *Love Is the Killer App* reminds us all that there's more to business than the bottom line."

—**TOM KELLEY**, author of *The Art of Innovation*

"This clever, creative, yet immensely practical book beautifully illustrates Carl Rogers's profound insight, 'That which is most personal is most general.'"

—**DR. STEPHEN R. COVEY**, author of
The 7 Habits of Highly Effective People

"Tim Sanders creates a new term for the business lexicon called 'lovecat,' which defines new ground rules for succeeding in today's challenging business environment. *Love Is the Killer App* offers an easy-to-follow road map with new twists on how to use and share information, add power to networks, and help people succeed by 'showing love.' The end result is that Tim Sanders shows us how to build ourselves as an outstanding brand—marketing advice that will create winners in any business setting."

—**PIERRE GAGNON**, president and chief operating officer, Mitsubishi Motor Sales of America

"You can throw away your ulcer medication. Tim Sanders has brought sanity and compassion into the workplace. He deftly guides our hearts to a notion that lingered somewhere in the distant past. 'Do unto others as you would have others do unto you.' The Golden Rule for a new century: Love is and always will be the killer app." —**JOHN RATZENBERGER**, actor and chairman and founder of Big Red Tent

"Tim's insightful book puts a bullet in the long-standing myth you have to be a jerk to be successful in business. On the contrary, he shows how you can 'give the love' while being successful. I'm proud to be a lovecat disciple."

—**MICHAEL ROBERTSON**, chairman of MP3.com

"With the same enthusiasm and provocative style as his live presentations, Sanders's book mixes one part universal truth, one part original observation, seasoned with sound bites from some of today's best business thinkers. It's definitely worth a taste."

—**JIM NOTARNICOLA**, chief marketing officer of Blockbuster, Inc.

"Tim Sanders's fresh new look at what truly drives the business world should spark a new trend in offices and corporations around the country. Instead of focusing on technology as the driver of success, this dot-com executive looks at people. He celebrates an inquisitive, compassionate spirit, and has a simple, powerful message that should resonate in every corner of our work and personal lives."

—**FAITH POPCORN**, founder of BrainReserve, Inc., and author of *EVEolution* and *Dictionary of the Future*

"Those seeking to perform at their best on the personal stage of business need look no further than Tim Sanders's outstanding book. It's easily digested and even more easily applied. If you follow its basic principles you can't help but lift up those around you, and your own career."

—**B. JOSEPH PINE II**, coauthor of
The Experience Economy: Work Is Theatre & Every Business a Stage

"It's hard not to get swept up by the rose-colored glow of this gleaming 'bizlove' philosophy, where people are excited to come to work and where they give out hugs and encouragement to everyone they come across. Sanders's brand of intelligent enthusiasm will . . . charm the wolves into submission"

—*Publishers Weekly*

"A new brand of inspiration . . . Sanders made a name for himself by navigating audiences through the uncharted and often turbulent waters of the new economy."

—*American Way*

"Lead 'em with love . . . *Love Is the Killer App* [is] a knowledgeable book that should win readers . . . this book should be required reading. Sanders relates, with witty and sharp stories, the way he has translated the love philosophy into his own life and business and put the positive vibe into others. This book is not just for the hip but for anyone who wants to positively turn relationships into job success."

—*Bookpage*

"[*Love Is the Killer App*] is about how to further oneself by sharing knowledge, networks, and compassion. I couldn't put it down."

—**DAVID BERKOWITZ**, *Emarketer* magazine

"Don't worry, be App-y. Lovecats, whether or not you inhabit the bizworld, you'll want to own this book."

—*Constant Reader*

"Thank you for writing *Love Is the Killer App*. I truly believe that this book will change my life. For me this is probably the most significant book I have read since Dale Carnegie's *How to Win Friends and Influence People*. That book helped me to see things from the other persons point of view and started me on the road to becoming a loving person."

—Mike Constant,
an engineer from Hampshire, England

"I've never felt moved enough after reading a book to write to the author, but I felt I had to in this case. I absolutely loved it. It's completely changed the way I think about business and life. I read every business book I can get my hands on, but this one was just so unlike anything I've read. I can't stop thinking about it. I've read about half the books on your recommended list and I can't wait to get stuck into the others. I'm driving everyone mad over here telling them about it. I've never given a book away as a present but I'm giving a copy to all my employees and close business contacts who I know will be really moved by it."

—Michael Smith,
a CEO from London, England

"Just wanted to thank you for writing *Love* . . . and sharing your knowledge. Your book has profoundly changed the way I'm dealing with developing myself and my new company. The methods outlined in your book are the Rosetta Stone I was needing. I just purchased several more copies of your book for my coworkers and friends."

—Hal Honigsberg,
a film editor from Los Angeles, California

"[*Love Is the Killer App*] put a name on something that I have been doing for years. Thanks again for validating those of us who already have chosen to live our lives this way, and for opening the eyes of others to the fact that there is a better way to live a successful life."

—Jeff Beamsley,
a software business development
professional from Monroe, Michigan

"Reading your book was like looking in the mirror . . . I see many similarities in our mindsets, but you have taken business life to another level. A level I aspire to reach. I made a decision at the first of the year to make some changes. Your book came to me as I've been moving in a new direction. It's very encouraging to think that I'm already on the right track."

—Pat Coyle,
a company president from Chicago, Illinois

THREE
RIVERS
PRESS

TIM SANDERS

How to Win Business and Influence Friends

LOVE IS THE KILLER APP

Published by Three Rivers Press, New York, New York.
Member of the Crown Publishing Group,
a division of Random House, Inc.
www.randomhouse.com

Originally published in hardcover by Crown Publishers,
a division of Random House, Inc., in 2002.

THREE RIVERS PRESS and the Tugboat design are registered
trademarks of Random House, Inc.

Printed in the United States of America

Design by Barbara Sturman

Library of Congress Cataloging-in-Publication Data
Sanders, Tim.
    Love is the killer app: how to win business and influence
friends / by Tim Sanders.—1st ed.
    1. Success in business.   2. Business networks.   I. Title.
HF5386.S323   2002
650.1—dc21   2001042466

ISBN 1-4000-4683-1

10 9 8 7 6

First Paperback Edition

To my wife, Jacqueline,

who is my stronghold

and the love of my life

CONTENTS

xi

Chris had worked with me for only a few weeks when I invited him to join a roundtable meeting with several outside consultants. He sat through the two-hour presentation stony-faced and silent until asked by the lead consultant if he had any comments. Then he nodded impatiently.

"This has been totally bush-league," he said. "I can't believe that we actually pay you to do this."

He went on to point out many serious flaws in the consultants' research, but he wasn't watching carefully enough to see the color drain from the consultants' faces. By the time they'd slunk out of the room, Chris had embarrassed me and everyone else present. He didn't quite figure this out until the next month's meeting, to which he pointedly wasn't invited.

Had Chris been smarter and nicer, he would have made his excellent points and become a hero for it. Poor Chris. He was armed to the teeth, well educated and wired for decision speed. But he was completely misdirected about how to use his many talents because he was also wired for war—always hostile, always battle-ready. He believed that success in business meant that you crush the weak. You always win. You disdain people who aren't as smart as you. You protect everything you know—and everyone you know—lest your weapons fall into enemy hands.

I dubbed him Mad Dog, and the name stuck.

Still, there was something beneath Chris's surface that was truly sweet. In an off-moment, when his defenses were down, he would flash a glimmer of tenderness, a ray of goodness. It was his tough background more than his personality that was making him mean. And he was smart enough to realize that his behavior was his Achilles' heel. His world stayed small while others around him were growing their networks before his eyes. He was having a bad ride in his career vehicle.

On top of that, he was miserable. Although he liked his actual work, he was unhappy in the workplace. He felt lost. He was doing what he had been told to do—Win at All Cost—but it didn't *feel* like winning.

I told Chris that his attitude was dangerous and that if he didn't believe me, he only had to watch how others treated him. He admitted that he'd been repeatedly taken off projects, and he now realized that his peers disliked him. One day he sent me this e-mail: "I have to change.

I'm out of step. I'm acting like someone from my father's generation."

Chris had approached me because he saw that the company listened to me and supported my projects; he knew that people thrived around me, that my network seemed to grow day to day and exponentially quarter to quarter. Chris was ready to listen.

"What do I do?" he asked.

"Be a lovecat," I replied. "And that means: Offer your wisdom freely. Give away your address book to everyone who wants it. And always be human."

I then told him about the advantages of being a lovecat, and the three necessary steps to getting there: sharing your knowledge, sharing your network, sharing your compassion.

We went right to work. First I helped him organize his reading. Chris didn't have a lot to offer that was portable to people—he could tell you what was wrong but he couldn't help make it right. His learning habits were screwed up. He'd taken such hard subjects in school that the moment he finished his graduate work, he stopped studying. He read only to get him through sleepless nights in his spartan Silicon Valley apartment. So I put him on a new curriculum. Reading is a source of potency, I said, so manage it like an asset. Become a walking encyclopedia of answers for anyone who has questions.

Then I showed him how to share his network. Because he was young, Chris didn't have many contacts. But he had the potential to make new ones; he was dealing with dozens of people on a weekly basis. Soon he was organizing internal meetings for his peers, pollinating them with new ideas he'd picked up from his reading and giving them access to his newly found contacts. Recently I saw him walk out of a twenty-person meeting that he had chaired masterfully, just months after wondering how he would ever get airtime at these gatherings. He had built his own little nest.

Mostly we talked about the third step: compassion, or the willingness to demonstrate your humanity at the office. At first Chris resisted because he thought it sounded trite, but the more he thought it over, the more he saw the light. Last month I received an e-mail from him saying, "Guess what? I just made someone's year." Chris had befriended a woman who worked in a section that was politically at risk. Chris opened up to the woman, whom he admired but had never told, letting her know how great she was at her job, and how valued her contributions were, at the time when she most needed support.

"I will help you," he said. "I will tell people how excellent you are. You should feel secure."

Those words turned her around. She was able to calm herself, which improved her work performance. And it gave Chris such a profound sense of satisfaction that he finally began to enjoy the office environment. He felt he belonged. He felt a sense of purpose.

Today I see a more potent Chris. I see a monster of knowledge, a connector of people, and the kind man who always existed within him, deep inside. Chris has changed his brand. He's found a way to use love more than hate. He is no longer Mad Dog. He is a lovecat. And being a lovecat is exactly what all of us must do if we want to succeed in the twenty-first century. Read on.

I

THE LOVECAT WAY

Not long ago, after I had delivered a speech on the new economy, a woman entering the job market approached me to talk about her career anxiety.

"I'm not worried that I won't land something good," she explained. "I'm afraid that work will be too cold and impersonal. What can I do to guarantee I'll be successful but also happy?"

The answer? The same advice I gave Chris: "Be a lovecat."

At a large sales conference last month, I met two men, one in accounting, the other in management; both of them were afraid. It wasn't that they feared the changes going on around them—they feared being left out of them.

"How do I drill into this World Wide Web thing?" one of them asked. "I don't know what to work on because this isn't my skill set. Am I still relevant? Is there anything I have to offer that can add value?"

The other man said, "I don't think I can compete

with these kids flying out of schools loaded with their new-economy knowledge and jargon. Everyone else seems to be jumping into new roles, but I think the world is limiting me with all its rules and biases."

"That's not how the world is run," I replied. "It's run via intangibles—knowledge, networks, and compassion."

It never seems to change. No matter how and where I meet these people, and no matter what their age or experience level, I have found one common truth: Men and women across the country are trying desperately to understand how to maintain their value as professionals in the face of rapidly changing times.

Until recently, bizpeople could survive for years without advice, without connection skills, perhaps even without new ideas. But now that the bizworld is moving at a velocity once unheard of, many of us can't keep up. We've made some bad decisions, we've received some bad advice, we didn't get connected to the right opportunities, we're feeling left behind or left out.

Technology has revolutionized our landscape. Before the information revolution, business changed gradually and business models became antiquated even more slowly. The value progression evolved over decades and double decades. You could go to college, get an M.B.A. and work for forty years, and your pure on-the-job knowledge stayed relevant. Relationships were for the most part geo-bound, and only a handful of people comprised your entire business network.

That was yesterday. Forget about today, because tomorrow is upon us. And to succeed in tomorrow's workplace, you need a killer application. (What's a killer app? There's no standard definition, but basically it's an excellent new idea that either supersedes an existing idea or establishes a new category in its field. It soon becomes so popular that it devastates the original business model.)

What is that application? Simply put: **Love is the killer app.** Those of us who use love as a point of differentiation in business will separate ourselves from our competitors just as world-class distance runners separate themselves from the rest of the pack trailing behind them.

This isn't just a feel-good message that I sense audiences want to hear. I believe that the most important new trend in business is the downfall of the barracudas, sharks, and piranhas, and the ascendancy of nice, smart people—because they are what I call lovecats. They will succeed for all the reasons you will discover in this book.

But first, what do I mean by *love*?

The best general definition I have ever read is in the noted philosopher and writer Milton Mayeroff's 1972 book *On Caring*: "Love is the selfless promotion of the growth of the other." When you are able to help others grow to become the best people they can be, you are being loving—and you, too, grow.

Mayeroff actually used the word *caring* more often than the word *love,* although *love* is interchangeable with such terms as *caring, charity,* and *compassion.* But because "Show me the love" has such a ring to it in a business context, *love* is the word I prefer to use.

Mayeroff, however, talked mostly about love in our personal lives. We need a different definition for love in our professional lives.

When we start a job, whether as recent graduate or CEO, we take on a contract to create more value than the dollar amount we are paid. If we don't add value to our employer, we are value losses; we are value vampires. My definition of added-value: **The value with you inside a situation is greater than the value without you.**

In your personal life, you can make decisions based on personal needs. If you wish to remain friendly with a toxic person, you have every right to do so. But business is not personal. Love in the bizworld is not some sacrificial process where we must all love one another come what may. There is no free love in the new economy. Every member of your team depends on each and every other member to contribute. You can't afford to take on people who will sink your value boat. So the definition of *love* must be modified to guarantee that it means not only you, but all the people who populate your bizworld, are value-added for that bizworld.

Here, then, is my definition of love business: **the act of intelligently and sensibly sharing your intangibles with your bizpartners.**

What are our intangibles? They are our **knowledge,** our **network,** and our **compassion.** These are the keys to true bizlove.

Who are our bizpartners? Potentially, they are each and every person in our work life, whether our bosses or bankers, our clients or competitors, the money guys with the cash to burn, the writers who spin it up so the stocks can churn.

In the following three chapters we will discuss each of the three intangibles in detail, but here they are in short form:

By **knowledge,** I mean everything you have learned and everything you continue to learn. Knowledge represents all you have picked up while doing your job, and all you have taught yourself by reading every moment you can find the time. It means every piece of relevant data and information you can accumulate. You can find knowledge almost anywhere—through observation, experience, or conversation. But by far the easiest, most efficient way to obtain knowledge is through books.

Think of your brain as a kind of piggy bank. Smart people fill it up with all they learn until they possess a formidable wealth of knowledge. Then there are those who sit around all day and never put anything in their bank; all they accumulate is a large butt. You see these people every day, on planes, trains, and in lounges, staring off into space, downing cocktails, heading off to business meetings ill-prepared. Like kids who don't know how to put pennies in their banks, these adults don't know how to accumulate knowledge.

When I give a speech, I often tell my audience that if they feel I have anything valuable to say, they should consider this: My knowledge isn't inherent. I wasn't born with an IQ of 200. I haven't started a colossal business. I am not a rocket scientist. Six years ago my career path wasn't any more remarkable than anyone else's. Then I went on a reading tear. And the more I read, the more I went into business meetings and won people's hearts—and their business, too.

So what I say to my audiences is: Don't let a guy like me get a step up on you. Maybe you've been in business for twenty-five years. Maybe you have stuff on your résumé

I would die for. Yet you're stopping in the race to let me catch up. And it's all because I keep reading.

I can't tell you how often people ask me after a speech, "Could you give me your book list? I should have been doing this for the last thirty years."

Says Harry Beckwith in *The Invisible Touch*: "Instead of thinking about value-added, think about knowledge-added. What knowledge can you add to your service, or communicate about your service, that will make you more attractive to . . . business partners and customers?"

✳

By **network,** I mean your entire web of relationships. In the twenty-first century, our success will be based on the people we know. Everyone in our address book is a potential partner for every person we meet. Everyone can fit somewhere in our ever-expanding business universe.

Relationships are the nodes in our individual network that constitute the promise of our bizlife and serve as a predictor of our success. Some of the brightest new-economy luminaries, such as Kevin Kelly (*New Rules for the New Economy*), or Larry Downes and Chunka Mui (*Unleashing the Killer App*), argue that companies, organizations, and individuals comprise, and are most highly valued for, their web of relationships. If you organize and leverage your relationships as a network, you will generate long-lasting value (and peace of mind) beyond your stock options, mutual funds, and bank accounts. You will also create a value proposition for new contacts, which in turn drives membership in that network—the prime law of business ecosystems, known as the Law of Network Effects. Value explodes with membership, and the value explosion sucks in more members, compounding the result. These famous wise words put it more succinctly: Them that's got, gets.

But not all of us know to go out and get. Try out this metaphor: When we are born, we receive a fishing net. Throughout our lives we troll for contacts—while in school, at work, or through professional organizations and clubs. If we are fishing well, we accumulate a network of people who support us, who appreciate our value, who lead us to new opportunities. But not all of us use our net wisely. While some of us fill our nets with prizewinning fish, others let their nets languish and fall to the bottom of the ocean, stuffed only with the deadweight of old tires.

Those of us who end up with the best-stocked net have a most valuable commodity. When we are fully and totally networked, we are powerful. Alone, even with all the wisdom in the world, we are powerless: castaways adrift in an impersonal ocean. Without a network, knowledge is nearly useless. Knowledge is your power source or your battery, but relationship is your nerve center, your processor. You get value from your knowledge, but it becomes real when you share it with your network.

I believe that Silicon Valley's greatest innovation is not the invention of wowie-zowie hardware and software, but the social organization of its companies and, most important, the networked architecture of the region itself—the complex web of former jobs, intimate colleagues, information leakage from one firm to the next, rapid company life cycles, and the agile e-mail culture.

Once, scarcity created value. Today abundance can create value. In the old days, when we traded tangibles such as gold, the less gold that was available, the higher its value. Supply-and-demand ruled. Now the opposite can be true. Abundance creates power. If you have a great idea for running a business, and it is adapted throughout your industry, your idea is more, not less, valuable. Value today derives from an idea that everyone has accepted, and then competition sets in to perfect the execution of that idea.

The more people in your network, the more powerful the network.

✳

By **compassion**, I mean that personal quality that machines can never possess—the human ability to reach out with warmth, whether through eye contact, physical touch, or words. The ability to show compassion is paramount to human happiness in any situation, whether at work or at home. You can't love a computer or a software program or even a book as you can love another person. Sometimes you just need a human.

The beauty of compassion is that every one of us already possesses it. We are born with our arms reaching out to embrace. Unlike knowledge and networks, which we build over time, we all can tell people how much we care about them. We can smile gently, and slap others on the back. We can hug, and we can listen quietly and, at a sad story's conclusion, say, "I truly feel for you."

At the office, our humanity can be defined as the ability to involve ourselves emotionally in the support of another person's growth. Whether we celebrate someone's accomplishments, or show true sympathy for someone's undoing, it's our warmth that separates us from the thinking machines.

How we are perceived as human beings is becoming increasingly important in the new economy. There was a time when people could sit back and play head games behind closed doors. There was a time when people who were unsympathetic, mean-spirited, or unkind could feel secure knowing little could be done about it. The new economy doesn't allow for this. There are two major reasons why.

The first is choice. Choice spells doom for villains.

Let's say that, twenty-five years ago, you were working in an area where there was only one place to buy a great cup of coffee. The guy who served it was a coffee Nazi, but you had no option, so you went to his deli every day even though you hated him. Today, however, there may be a dozen coffee places within a stone's throw. Now if that man bothers you, you sample the competition's coffee, you find a substitute, you move on.

Likewise, twenty-five years ago, when you worked for a bad boss, you didn't have many tools with which to choose another job. There was the Sunday paper, your network of a few friends and family members, and that was about it. You stayed at that job longer than you wanted to because you truly believed you didn't have an alternative. Today, however, there are all kinds of new services that didn't exist in your parents' generation, aimed at helping you locate and change jobs. You don't have to put up with the same head games they did. A fresh start is a mouse click away. If your boss is smart, he or she is fully aware of this.

The second reason the new economy is inhospitable to noxious people is what I call the New Telegraph. In the Old West, communications technology in the form of telegraph wires changed the composition of commercial life. It taught merchants that they had to be decent. Before the telegraph, scamming someone wasn't difficult. My

Granny Hattie, who was in her late eighties when I was a child, told me about an old relative of ours who used to sell some miracle cleanser that was basically an inexpensive soap solution packaged as a fancy cure-all. He did well simply by moving to the next county if anyone wised up to his gimmick. But he went out of business once the telegraph wires went up, because the word that he was a snake-oil salesman traveled faster than he could.

That same phenomenon has now gone global and real time. If someone rips you off, all kinds of great technology are available to let others know, from planetfeedback.com to just plain e-mail. A truly bad boss is his own worst viral marketer.

It doesn't matter what industry you're in—you have more choices and more information at your disposal. So when you don't like certain people, it's easier than ever to escape them.

As the world becomes more competitive, we also compete for people's emotions. In business, to paraphrase National Basketball Association commissioner David Stern, it's not completely important what people think about you—it is, however, totally important how they feel about you.

People are hungry for compassion. There's never enough of it. And the tougher the times are, the more important it becomes. If we dot.communists had a bible, it would preach that the network was created in the image of men and women. No matter how technical our workstations may be, because we are all human, the network is at its best when compassion underlies our motivation.

❋

Knowledge, network, compassion: These are the intangibles you share with those you have chosen as your partners. These are the values that can drive your career to the top or over the top—they'll take you wherever you want to go. They certainly have taken me where I wanted to go, because, as I'll explain, *Show you the love* is exactly what I do as a business lovecat.

I'm not alone in this. Over and over I have discovered that the people in the bizworld who are most successful, and happiest, are the lovecats. These are the people whom you always like the most, the ones who are most passionate from 9 to 5, or 8 to 10, or whatever their hours. They are the ones who are most generous with their knowledge, their address book, and their compassion.

Take a second and close your eyes. Visualize the happiest and the most successful bizpeople you've ever met. (Remember, I said "happiest.") Are they smart? Generous? Kind? More than nine out of ten times I hear "Yes!"

Every day, high-priced consultants are telling their

executive-level manager clients that they must go out, build, and monetize their intangibles. But I don't think this concept of intangibles should belong just to people at the highest levels. It should belong to everyone, whether at the top of the management team or at an entry-level position.

The fact is, the old, loveless way won't get you anywhere in today's economy. Current bizpractice is too heavily influenced by books that tell you how to swim with the sharks or eat with the barracudas. These philosophies may occasionally promote a disingenuous appearance of caring, but they are actually grounded in an attitude of material gain. It's all about predatory marketing, capturing market share, first-mover advantage, preemptive marketing strategy, category killers. These are the mantras of the airport gift shop books that litter the minds of today's bizfolk.

I know this because I've read them all. Corporate page turners. You win, they lose, it's over. I've always warned consultant friends that they could get fired if their client CEO reads the wrong book on the plane: He stops to buy a tin of Altoids, picks up one of those cutthroat management tomes, and lands at O'Hare a changed man. He doesn't waste much time as he hoses two deals because he now thinks he sees things for what they really are, and they don't fit what he just read.

This bizcommunity currently describes its results in

terms of winning and market-share recovery. But that's the same value prop from ten years, maybe ten decades, ago. We all now know that reality is changing. And some very brave companies, such as Cisco Systems, already measure themselves by the quality of their relationships with their customers rather than by victories over their competitors. Salespeople make their bonuses based in large part on customer satisfaction instead of gross sales or profit. Cisco is applying love to the workplace and profiting from it—just as I, too, am profiting. The fact is, my own career would never have taken off without those basic intangibles.

When I was nine years old, the members of my congregation at our Clovis, New Mexico, church used to call me "the little reverend." I would become highly excited whenever I watched our congregation mesmerized by a sermon or homily. I would memorize it, evangelize it, and experiment with it. To me, a minister moving the flock was as thrilling as any magician pulling a rabbit out of a hat. This was all done with emotions and words!

When you're only nine, and you grasp what the preacher is saying, the church lets you run with it. I'd hop up on the stage, recite the books of the Bible, play the piano, and sing. But before I did, I'd take a sermon on charity, for example, and chat about it like a young Steve

Allen casually gabbing by his Steinway. One of my favorite topics centered on missionaries. My grandmother always gave them money whenever they came through town, even when times were tight. "Yet," I would thunder, "most of you out there are constantly rewarding yourselves with a big meal or a new car and never give a cent to these poor people. Do you ever reach into your purse or pocket and give away the few pennies they're asking for? Who is to say that our own personal mission is more important than the work of God?"

As I grew older, I channeled that mini-minister energy into other activities. I became a high school and collegiate debater, leading my junior-college team to several national championships. I then won a scholarship to Loyola University and a fellowship at the University of Arizona, and eventually a law school scholarship. But I turned it all down to carry my zeal into the entertainment business, where I worked as a musician.

Because I found reggae superstar Bob Marley the ultimate minister—he used dazzling music to heal and teach—my first love was reggae. I traveled around the country with a band, living out of vans, playing whenever we could land a gig, until I settled in Dallas. There I got the bug for a mix of industrial music combined with Native American. By this time my wife, Jacqueline, had joined me in founding a new four-member band; I was the lead singer and also hacked out computer programming synchronized to the show.

Eventually Jacqueline and I tired of the musician's life, although we still perform today as a hobby.

I next went into marketing in the early 1990s at a video-production studio. I was good at sales but the process made me unhappy. I didn't know why at the time. I just felt stuck and wanted out. Eventually I took off for a cable-television company where the work was interesting but the place itself wasn't. There was no love there, just a great deal of fear and loathing. I spent five years as a sales manager in this disagreeable environment where the bosses felt all employees were liars unless proven otherwise; there was so much distrust that we weren't allowed to enter or leave the building with anything but purses and wallets, for fear of theft. As a sales manager, I held court over twenty salespeople. Since the owners always arrived late, every morning I had a brief bully pulpit on how to humanize the job. I tried to take that weird business and spin it up to help these people. Perhaps here I learned that even in a bad environment you can still have a good heart.

And, I was given a chance to learn about the Internet. The 4 A.M. cable program I was producing wasn't reaching an audience, so out of desperation I started studying a new phenomenon called streaming video (broadcasting video over the Internet). Through my research I met the people at Broadcast.com, a start-up that was blazing the streaming-video way, and in 1997 they offered me a job as an account executive.

Finally I'd found a company with excellent values. Broadcast.com's CEO, Mark Cuban, had a motto: "Make love, not war." Not original, but to me it felt like the elixir of life. Mark passionately believed that customers should be happy, even if that meant our working twenty-four hours a day. I'd never known anyone like that before. I was thrilled. It was freedom, baby! I dedicated myself to learning how to please customers no matter what it took; the hours, the work, and the sweat didn't matter. What mattered were the relationships I was building.

I'd been at Broadcast.com only a few months when I began to formulate my lovecat system—but it took me some time even to realize that I was doing it. When I worked as a musician, it hadn't occurred to me to share the love. My day jobs weren't serious. They paid the rent— no more, no less. When you are a hired gun, you kill on contract, you don't take a hit for the team. If I wanted to make a connection with a bizmate, I would invite him or her to hear me play music at night. It didn't occur to me to be nice to them at work.

Meanwhile, I was searching for my own personal killer app—the stratagem that would make me successful in the workplace (although at the time I still hadn't heard the actual phrase "killer app"). Never having had a job that truly mattered to me, I wasn't sure what it would be. Maybe tenacity? So I put time and effort into being successful, working fourteen hours a day, making hundreds of cold phone calls. Or maybe it was shrewdness in negotiation? So I carefully studied the other sales executives who used chess moves and Vulcan mind games while bargaining.

At the same time, aware that I needed to learn more about business, I began stuffing my plate with books. When one of my Broadcast.com littermates, Karl Meisenbach, found this out, he recommended *Net Gain* by John Hagel and Arthur Armstrong.

Net Gain describes the creation of virtual communities and their extraordinary potential. The owners of these online communities will, according to the authors, extract great wealth because an online community is valuable to both the creator *and* the member—the member receives personalized attention, and the creator gets to customize content in a way that can't be done in print, based on an increasing knowledge of the member, which in turn makes it even more valuable to the member as that knowledge grows. And because this is all done online, it costs less than catalogs, which are subject to the rising costs of printing and shipping.

I ate the book up like it was candy, or better—candy that was excellent for you.

One day in late 1998, not long after I had finished the book, the phone rang. It was Ken Weil, a vice president at Victoria's Secret, making calls to explore the costs of broadcasting a lingerie fashion show over the Internet.

Ken, a smart and capable bizperson, clearly wanted a price and only a price, but I started selling him on the concepts in *Net Gain* and the new kind of business model it would entail, which I felt was more important than finding the lowest broadcast fees. *Net Gain* makes the argument that information is money: If you manage people's information, you are managing their money. There's nothing more strategic in the new economy than building a database of your customers' profiles and managing it carefully. The trick is getting the customers to give you that information in the first place.

Ken wanted a good deal. I wanted to evangelize. Still, my company was in the business of making money, so we set up a conference call: me, my boss, Ken Weil, and Tim Plzak, a vice president at Victoria's Secret's parent company who was also the IT (information technology) director.

Never having done this before, I was nervous, which

meant we had to rehearse until we got it right. We even role-played. My boss, Stan Woodward, acted as Ken and asked me hard questions, some so tough that I had to run to my desk, get the book, read my notes, and then dash back to Stan without letting him know I'd been rereading. But when I finally made Stan a believer, I had the confidence to pick up the phone.

It was the call of my life. In it I reviewed chunks of theory from *Net Gain,* but this time I made it clearer that it wasn't just an idea, but a practical concept that could make Victoria's Secret a great deal of money. I showed how this fashion show could create an immense database that would allow an extraordinarily inexpensive conversation between the company and all the digitally aroused customers who would log on and give Victoria's Secret their online addresses—people who were much more likely to keep track of their e-mail than their snail mail. Victoria's Secret, I said, was stuck with a blue-snail addiction: They were acting like an Old World company that hires a printing press and relies on the post office (whose letter carriers are snails in blue uniforms) every time they want to reach customers.

I also sent the book itself to Ken.

Ken got it. He saw the value proposition in using the fashion show as a draw for customer information—the new black gold, the new Texas tea. So at the end of the day, although we didn't submit the lowest bid, we won the business because I had shared my new knowledge. We had added intangible value.

The fashion show took place on February 2, 1999. Some in the media called it a technical failure because many people who tried to log on couldn't; a few newspapers mocked the technology, and *Saturday Night Live* even staged a parody. But for us and for Victoria's Secret, it was an overwhelming success—the biggest event in the history of the Internet at the time, with more than one million people logging in to watch an eighteen-minute Web segment. Victoria's Secret ended up with the names and e-mail addresses of more than a half million current and potential customers. That was the business model, and that's what made them so happy.

When the event was over, Ken told me it was the most awesome experience of his life, and he wrote a letter to Mark Cuban saying so, a letter I still have over my desk. (Mark was so pleased he framed it in gold leaf and left it in my cubicle as a surprise. Mark loves happy customers. That's why I dig him.)

That spring, Victoria's Secret decided to stage a second event. Now the goal was to make sure that it was a great user experience, which meant we couldn't tolerate any technical glitches. So when Ken told me that I had to make sure that more people could log on, I committed myself to facilitating an unholy alliance between Broadcast.com and what I call the co-opetition, America Online and Microsoft, to pull it off. ("Co-opetition" comes from the book of the same name by Adam M. Brandenburger, Barry J. Nalebuff, and Ada Brandenberger; it refers to the situation that develops when competitors cooperate for the greater good. Or, as Microsoft's Bill Gates says: Sometimes the lambs just have to lie down with the wolves.)

It was the first time I'd been willing to share my growing network with reckless abandon and without expectations. We held a summit where Victoria's Secret was able to talk to everyone else prior to signing a contract with us. I even left the room so the other companies could strategize networking and distribution plans together; these independent and unbrokered relationships were necessary to carry the load of VicSecret2.

But instead of teaming up with someone else (and, yes, others did try to outbid us), Victoria's Secret stayed put because, they told us, we had been willing to share our knowledge and our network to make everything work for their benefit.

We had shared the third intangible, compassion, too. However, this took more time. After the first event I flew to Columbus, Ohio, to meet with Ken and do a postmortem.

It was a nasty, snowy day, and I had one of those runny, drippy, slobbery colds; my plane was late, the ride from the airport was terrible, and I felt as low as I could go. But the moment Ken saw me, his eyes lit up like a Christmas tree and he gave me a warm hug. Now this was not the kind of man from whom you would expect an embrace—Ken is a great man, but a reserved one.

Here was the third part of my system. During that two-month relationship, Ken and I had become more than friends. I was his champion. If he needed something— public relations, technology, or information—I bled pink. (Sometimes you bleed the color of your customer, and Victoria's Secret's color is pink—Compaq's is red, IBM's blue, Yahoo!'s purple.) I showed Ken love before I had even realized it—I told him how much I was cheering for him in his new job (he'd had it for only three weeks prior to our first conversation). I told him how much I liked him as a person and which attributes I particularly appreciated. I was always careful to double-shake his hand and add a shoulder pat, which was as much touch as I felt he could handle. I committed all of my intangible resources to the man, introducing him to as many key Broadcast.com staffers, including Mark Cuban, as made sense.

I began using the word *love* openly in conversations. "There's got to be some love here," I would say. "Show me some love." And they used the word back at me. When Ken called to discuss an important technical issue regarding the next broadcast, he said right off, "We'll need some of that love."

Right then and there I knew! Love was indeed the answer.

VicSecret2 took place in May of 2000 in France, at the site of the Cannes Film Festival, where Ken had invited Jacqueline and me to help coordinate the final details.

Meanwhile, still on my knowledge tear, I now focused my evangelism on Tim Plzak. Since this fashion show intended to deliver rich information, it was thought of as a technology issue. So I spread a new idea to Tim based on John McKean's *Information Masters,* a book about information competency and priorities—i.e., the percentage of financial and resource priorities a company must put into its information systems, hardware, software, staff, culture, and organization. McKean posits that most companies misjudge their priorities; they think it's all about hardware and software. Wrong. Success in the future will be based on the fuzzy intangibles: the way you speak as a leader, the culture you nurture, the processes for managing information you set up for your people, the partnerships you form around technology's opportunities and challenges. Put your efforts into the people and the fabric of your company, and you, too, can become an information master.

This book started us thinking about how to deploy a new technology called multicasting. Until now video programs on the Internet had been distributed like videotapes, one at a time, one copy for each user. Unicast video broadcasting is very taxing on computers, systems, and networks because it buckles the Net's resources while making virtual tapes at a rate of more than one thousand per second. Multicasting is more like radio and TV: The producer makes one copy and puts it on the Internet so that many can consume it at once. This represented a genuine solution for Victoria's Secret.

But we needed to build an alliance of several different players to realize the multicasting dream. Required for success were the participating people, companies, and their information systems—it wasn't just a matter of bandwidth, hardware, and software.

Ken and Tim signed off on the idea and it turned out to be the right way to go. Because this second show was multicasted with wide partner participation, almost everyone who wanted to see it was able to log on successfully. It was a huge triumph.

By this time we were all lovecats. We used the word "love" openly with each other and we meant it. We were talking to each other as we would to close friends. Ken began to share his intangibles with me, too. He gave me great insight on brand marketing, based on his knowledge from experience and books. He introduced me to his network, including Ed Razek, the president of Intimate Brands, Victoria Secret's parent company.

Compassion in business, I now knew, was not just possible—it was necessary. It was the splendid complement to knowledge and network, a holy trinity if ever I saw one. I realized my system for being the best possible lovecat was in place.

These last five years have reminded me of my time as the mini-minister because I am out evangelizing bizlove right and left. After Yahoo! bought Broadcast.com, I transferred to Northern California and founded Yahoo!'s ValueLab (although that took some time, as you will soon see). The ValueLab creates large partnerships with Fortune 500 companies. But we are also the company's thought leadership center, working evenings and weekends producing studies and presentations for the other Yahoo!s on how to grow into better businesspeople based on what we've learned. This work is not required, but we feel it's important to build a huge store of intangibles at the company.

I always try to preach what I practice. My fire never

disappeared; after years of hiding it has reemerged, no longer centered on religion, now focused on the bizworld. It seems to spring into action every time I see pain: the pain I notice when people and their companies are losing money; the pain individuals feel when they don't know how and where they fit in to the value chain; the pain that overcomes a friend who is one contact away from executing an incredible idea. I ache for people who, in the words of U2 singer Bono, "still haven't found what they are looking for." I see this kind of pain, the minister hat goes on, and I start thinking about big ideas.

But by being a good evangelist, I'm helping myself as well as helping others. I improve my own journey—and the journey of all the others around me—because bizlove has at least six considerable benefits for every potential lovecat.

BENEFIT 1: YOU BUILD AN OUTSTANDING BRAND AS A PERSON.

In the new economy, because you are valued and rewarded for your knowledge and your network rather than your seniority or your pedigree, everything can seem upside down if you've come up the traditional route.

But a successful brand will always give you powerful leverage. That goes for products, companies, and people: Whether it's Ivory soap, CNN, or Michael Jordan, build a brand so that people will trust you, like you, pursue you.

If you don't build a brand, you risk being commoditized—in other words, you risk becoming a human switch, someone who performs a function that has yet to be automated, but probably will be at some future date. And there are millions of you out there, you undifferentiated middle managers, you enterprise resource planners, you service providers. The moment some giant software concern can sell a program that switches that same switch you do, you're out of a job. You're a commodity that has been replaced by a cheaper one. As one of my mentors, bizguru Tom Peters, says, "Be distinct or be extinct."

The best response to this threat is to differentiate yourself. The good news is that there's no such thing as a commodity—only a person who thinks like one.

There are many formulas for how to stop thinking like a commodity and start accomplishing personal branding; my personal favorite is loosely adapted from Duane Knapp's remarkable book *The Brand Mindset*. It's organized around the acronym DREAM. You become a brand by realizing each step of the DREAM.

D stands for **Differentiation.**

Former Coca-Cola CEO Robert Goizueta once said, "In real estate, it's location, location, location. In business, it's differentiate, differentiate, differentiate."

This is the most important facet of building a brand. Since attention is scarce, anything that is differentiated extracts a premium price. To the extent I can differentiate my person, product, or service, I extract premium value. By becoming a knowledge guru, by sharing your vast network, and by being a compassionate bizpartner, you create a differentiated brand for yourself. You're useful, you're memorable, you're personable. People like you.

That's an important part of differentiation—it isn't just about being different. Sure, you could imitate basketball luminary Dennis Rodman and dye your hair pink. But that alone doesn't sustain itself. Differentiation is about being different in a positive, productive manner that can sustain itself over time, and the best way to do that is to offer up your intangibles to those with whom you wish to partner—because then what you offer truly lasts.

R stands for **Relevance.**

Bizlove is an act of intimacy. It's day love, which is like day trading, but here your currency doesn't consist of your stocks and bonds. It's you. After all, once upon a time we didn't buy stocks at work—we had brokers who called us before work in the morning or at the end of the day. We didn't build wealth beyond our jobs while still at our job. Then the Internet came along and trading stocks from our desktops became easy. Suddenly we were all creating wealth while we were earning wealth.

Just as the Internet offers that opportunity to day traders, bizlove offers that opportunity to workers. You can build relationships and be fed compassion while you're doing your job. It doesn't have to happen at night, over weekends, at churches, or at social events. We can all be day lovers now.

When you develop these kinds of ties with bizpeople, you become highly relevant to them. Relevance is determined to a large degree by the frequency with which something important appears in your life. Bread and milk are very relevant to most people's lives. Ferraris and orangutans are not.

If all I do as a bizperson is take what I can get from you, I'm not truly relevant to your life. You may have to speak to me now, but if I lose the job that brings us into contact, you probably won't speak to me again. But a good lovecat's relevance to others is a daily one: Everyone always needs to know something new, or needs to be connected to someone new, or needs an affirmation that he or she is a good person.

E is for Esteem.

People hold you in the highest esteem when they realize you have no expectations that you will receive anything in return for what you are willing to give.

Esteem comes down to trust. We aren't esteemed because we are competent as much as because we are trustworthy. When asked, the average person a hundred years ago said that the biggest problem in business was stealing. Today, it is lying. People value trust today more than ever before.

Whenever we offer up our intangibles, we become a mirror of other people's own self-image. Consider this: As I have become a bizlover, I have learned that people think I am just like them—because most people aspire to be smart, sweet, generous. So when you act that way, others think, "I like this guy—he/she is like me—a nice, smart person." That, in turn, creates high esteem, which means that bizlove not only helps people trust you, it helps them build a sense of trust in themselves as you mirror the parts of their personalities they like the most.

A is for **Awareness.**

Most people spend their time working their way down the food chain. When they're hired, or when they're brought into the company for a meeting, they may meet the vice president or the president or the CEO. Seldom will they see that top person again; typically they'll end up dealing with a lower-level manager.

Lovecats stray in the opposite direction. We may start

out talking with someone at a junior level, but we end up in the president's office—not because we have a deal to offer, but because sponsor after sponsor has said the same thing about us to the president: "You've got to meet this person."

When people realize that as a lovecat you are like an encyclopedia squared, that you have a Rolodex the size of your laptop, that you're passionate and kind, they become increasingly aware of who you are and what you can do. They soon start taking care of your marketing, creating awareness of a brand called U, because good news and good views travel with the speed of sound on the Internet.

M is for the **Mind's Eye.**

As Duane Knapp says, "In order to be a brand, a product or service must be characterized by a distinctive attribute in the consumer's mind." Companies spend millions of dollars for this kind of purchase intent. For example, Coca-Cola builds a brand that says "We refresh you." You hear that, you know that, and when you want to be refreshed, you buy a Coca-Cola. When we prefer a brand, we will buy it first, and we are even willing to pay more money.

Likewise, if we have a distinctive brand in the mind's eye of our bizmates, they will give us their best business opportunities. If we don't install ourselves, we lose that business. Let's say I make a promise to you to deliver great service. Then I betray it because I don't care enough, or because I have other items on my agenda. My promise no longer exists in your mind's eye. From now on, when I say "I promise," you hear "I don't promise."

The sincerity of my promise makes it real for others. People who don't install themselves remain peripheral, but a lovecat becomes an integral part of life.

I want others, when they think of people in my arena, to think of me first and to think of me immediately. And they will, because I have proven my value to them through my intangibles. I am the apple in their mind's eye. Most people have five credit cards in their wallet, but 80 percent of their purchases are made with the card at the top of the wallet. Lovecats will always become top-of-wallet for their bizpartners.

D for *differentiation*, *R* for *relevance*, *E* for *esteem*, *A* for *awareness*, and *M* for *mind's eye*. Put them together and they spell lovecat success.

BENEFIT 2: YOU CREATE AN EXPERIENCE.

The more you read, the more you know, and the more knowledge you have to pass along. I wouldn't be as familiar with this benefit of bizlove if I hadn't read Joseph Pine and James Gilmore's *The Experience Economy*.

According to Pine and Gilmore, there have been four phases of economic progression. The first was the commodity phase, where, after locating and extracting resources, people sold them in raw form: agriculture, energy, precious metals.

Next came the goods phase, which concerned manufacturing—people took commodities and organized them into products, meaning that you paid more for the product than you did for the raw materials that went into it (this was the birth of the concept "value-added"). Between the 1920s and 1970s, as has often been noted, many people worked for the well-known commodity generals: General Mills, General Electric, General Motors, General Dynamics, and so on.

The third phase was the service economy, which began in the 1970s and is just now ending. This phase centered on the creation of more than goods; it emphasized benefits over features. Companies were challenged to put service in every product and a product in every service, meaning that you became differentiated because you delivered a service apart from your goods. If you didn't, you faced ruin. For instance, in the early 1990s IBM almost went bankrupt (until it reemerged a thriving and powerful services business).

What happened? Dell happened, Gateway happened—companies in the business of delivering more than goods, companies that developed into service companies. The Dell computer wasn't necessarily better than the IBM. Its concept of serving the customer from beginning to end was.

The fourth phase of economic progression, which is just beginning now, is organized around the *experience*. According to Pine and Gilmore, smart companies are starting to "use their products as props and their services as a stage to deliver a compelling experience." Commodities were measured by their characteristics, goods by their features, services by their benefits, and now experiences by their sensations.

Here's an example adapted from the book to illustrate how the phases have progressed. When my mom was young, Grandma would bake her a birthday cake using raw materials—flour, sugar, eggs. It took half a day to make and cost less than a dollar. When I was a kid, my mother made a cake out of a boxed mix. What a deal for Mom! It cost about two dollars and took an hour. By the time I was a hyperactive teenager, she had moved over to stage three—she outsourced the cake to a local bakery for ten dollars. Today, when my own kid has a birthday, I have to stage an experience for him and his friends, whether that means a trip to Chuck E. Cheese, Disney Club, or Discovery Zone—and now the price tag is approaching one hundred dollars.

Even at the customer-service end of the operation, it's not enough simply to supply the service. The service has to be amusing, interesting, compassionate. Companies that create a positive experience are rewarded with loyalty and premium pricing, while companies paying attention only to the bottom line are not.

One of the best examples of the experience economy is chip maker Intel, which knows to stage an experience every time you touch their brand. Intel's goal is to make you forget that they manufacture computer chips. Through cobranding and audio branding, they create such a fun experience that, as CEO Andy Grove once said, people have "waves of lust" about the product without having to know what the product really is. It's true—most people know nothing about Intel chips, but they want them inside their computers because everything they do is fun, from the winning look of the logo and their auditory branding (the Intel chime is almost as famous as Big Ben's) to their use of the Blue Man Group to entertain prospective buyers via advertising.

Restaurants have also figured out how to exploit experience. Rainforest Café may not serve better food or offer better service, but it does provide a wonderful experience that means, when you're at the mall and wish you were someplace else, you can enter one of their restaurants and feel like you're on safari. You certainly pay for it, but at the end of the day, the experience is worthwhile.

Back during the Depression people worried about survival. Today the affluent worry about whether or not they are going to have a good experience. To quote rap musician Dr. Dre, "No more hard living, barbecues every day." Or, moving closer to home, my mother still worries about another Great Depression, whereas my stepson doesn't—his online screen name is CashSpenda.

When you represent knowledge, opportunity, self-lessness, and intimacy, you are not just a service provider or a product. You are fun, you are interesting, you are valu-able; you take people places they have never been before, you show them books they have never heard of, you intro-duce them to people they never dreamed they would meet—in short, you are the equivalent of a human theme park.

BENEFIT 3: YOU HAVE ACCESS TO PEOPLE'S ATTENTION.

Attention is one of the world's scarcest resources, and decision-maker attention is something companies are willing to spend billions of dollars to buy. According to Seth Godin's best-selling *Permission Marketing,* the average person is attacked by about three thousand marketing mes-sages every day, compared with the few hundred our parents endured. And that's just consumer messages—bizfolk are subjected to even more creative and noncreative intrusions than their parents by an exponential factor.

Attention is money. Think about television. When you build a television network, your first obligation is to go out and get eyeballs—you accumulate good content so viewers can't stop watching, until everyone is paying attention. You then rent that attention to advertisers. There's nothing more valuable than attention; this was true a hundred years ago when people spent their Sunday mornings over coffee reading newspapers filled with ads, and it's true today, when attention is scarcer than ever because we have so many more places to allocate it—print media, radio, television, our computer screens.

So if you think getting good ROI—Return On Investment—is important, you should also be thinking about ROA, or Return On Attention. Give us some of your undivided attention, lovecats say, and we will give you a high return against it. We will supply you with creativity, we will help unlock your imagination, we will build your network, we will give you a foundation for your business practice.

When people know that handing over their attention is valuable, they do it. You march right past the secretaries and the assistants and the associates and everyone else waiting in line. When you have the attention of others who are important, you are a deal maker. If I can get the attention 24/7, 365, of CEOs, or of my boss, or of my number-one supplier, I am rich with value.

Bizlove gets you attention. Others get only time. The difference between having their time and their attention is the difference between ham and eggs. The chicken is involved, but the pig is committed.

We are all multitaskers today. We don't perform just one activity at a time. While we are on the phone, we also scan our e-mail, whip up memos, read notes that are being slipped to us even as we do everything else. But when lovecats deal with people, they can stop the multitasking and get undivided attention because their value prop is high. This produces results that last.

BENEFIT 4: YOU HARNESS THE POWER OF POSITIVE PRESUMPTION.

All those debates I argued in school had two sides: affirmative and negative. The former would challenge some new law, policy, or program, and the latter would defend the status quo. Because of the inherent risk in any change, the negative side always went into battle armed with positive presumption—in other words, people tend to presume a proposal is bad until proven otherwise.

In the traditional bizworld, presumption is against you if you represent change, because people fear risk. But if you have a lovecat relationship with your bizpartners, you are armed with their trust and their respect. This allows you more leeway in helping them change.

Trying to change any bizperson is difficult. Trying to change someone who doesn't trust you is almost impossible.

Think about the hamburger. You're on a business trip in a strange city and you want to eat lunch. You drive to the nearest shopping center and you spot a familiar-looking chain restaurant as well as a small café called Bugs. Most of us don't take the chance. The burger we get from the chain restaurant may not be the best burger we've ever had, but we know it, we trust it, we'll eat it. Bugs may look pleasant, but we have no idea what it really offers. That's why businesses spend so much money to make us familiar with them and why they spend so much to make us like their product. Presumption rules in an attention-scarce economy.

The same goes for people. Because lovecats build relationships with a deep level of trust, people will presume our arguments are correct, our recommendations are solid, our referrals are valuable. They presume that we have their interests at heart. In the bizworld, this becomes an advantage capable of winning any debate.

BENEFIT 5: YOU RECEIVE EXCEPTIONAL FEEDBACK.

Before I became a lovecat, I was paid in the old-economy ways for my services. If I gave you some basic advice on how to run a company, you had to do something for me in return. If I set you up with a new client, you had to do something for me in return. The transaction went: I do my job, you pay me money.

Now, because I'm not always working for cash, because I often give away my services, I receive more than money in return. People are more inclined to tell me which of my ideas worked and which didn't. They tell me which of my contacts were helpful and which weren't. They know that I am on their side and that I am genuinely interested in the follow-up, so my relationship doesn't end when the business transaction ends. The relationship endures. People keep talking to me. They tell me what crashes, what craters, what flies, what soars.

For instance, at one point in my career I believed the old adage that first-mover advantage was everything—i.e., if you're first and fastest with an idea, you win. I evangelized the idea heavily until the CEO of one of the world's largest retail companies showed me that he was often fourth or fifth in the space because he wanted to wait to see how the idea worked. He used other factors, such as relationships or talent, to win. I dropped the first-mover idea from my repertoire.

This kind of feedback gives lovecats a huge advantage because we learn more about what happens when our advice is implemented. It's not academic. It's real. And from each example, intelligence grows. You know when to avoid a situation, you know when to sponsor it. You don't become a boo-boo (a Silicon Valley term for someone who has book knowledge but no practical experience).

There's more. Recipients of bizlove are more likely to give back in other ways. For instance, they recommend books and contacts. They give a heads-up on new companies and esoteric technologies. They make you feel good about yourself. And they expand your network. After all, to the extent you use your network, you grow your network.

BENEFIT 6: YOU GAIN PERSONAL SATISFACTION.

These are turbulent times. Depending on how we were raised, the schools we attended, the jobs our parents held, our expectations can start out sky high. But how many of us are living up to our hopes? Think of that guy who came from a prominent family, who was captain of his high school football team, who graduated from Stanford: Did he think that fifteen years later he'd be idling as an administrative manager at a software concern? Or as a perpetual middle-level executive at a manufacturing company? Or languishing on some creative team in an advertising department that's going nowhere? Of course not. If he knew that's where he'd be now, he would have been seriously freaked out fifteen years ago.

People once judged their careers in terms of rank, status, and money. If you worked at your company for a long time, you were more secure in your job, you had a higher rank, you were given privilege. As long as you followed the rules and you added a little value, you were paid well and set up for retirement.

The new economy has obliterated that model. Those rewards are no longer controlled by those who made the original promise. Their company was bought, someone bigger merged into it, the department was downsized.

Just the other day I was talking to Anna, an old friend who has always believed that success is a matter of achieving the proper goals: terrific grades at excellent schools, excellent jobs at solid companies. Anna did it all. She assumed this meant she was on the fast track to stardom. What Anna didn't realize was that fewer and fewer people cared about this path anymore. The reason for our conversation was that her employer had merged with a larger firm. Suddenly Anna found herself facing competition for her own job. Of all things, it turned out to be a contest based on who the new corporate entity thought would do the best job for the smallest salary. That wasn't a battle Anna had ever prepared for. Although her résumé glittered, she lost out to someone who could do the same job for less money. Anna doesn't understand how this happened and hasn't yet accepted my analysis of her situation; we'll need to talk about it more.

We live in an age where information is more important than seniority. In Silicon Valley, where I work, you get paid for what you know, not how long you've been around or where you went to college. That's good for some, bad for others. Like it or not, it's happening all across the country, in job after job.

For me, that piece of change is good. It brings me peace. It makes me more valuable than ever, because by building up my intangibles, I am creating much more worth than my position requires.

Anyway, my circle of friends never respected that other system, where your overall performance was judged as much by your golf game as by your ability to hit your quarterly numbers. Success in that system wasn't much to aspire to— not for those of us who wanted to build up our intangibles.

Bob Marley once said that he was tormented by his inability to fix everything. Sometimes that's how we feel about our careers. We are tormented by our potential. It never seems realized. We sense we could be doing better. But when I am out being a lover, a one-man value lab, I am at ease. I am not tormented by my potential; I am motivated by it, I am excited by it, I know I am developing it better than I ever could in that old world, where my potential meant so little and my golf score meant so much.

Every time I board an airplane I scan the cabin. I know these people; we're together several times a week, all clutching our carry-ons so we don't have to check our bags, herding together by the gate so we can rush like bulls to grab that overhead cabin space. Now and then I spot someone like myself and I try to start a conversation. But mostly I see beat-up, wearied, downcast folks coming off a weekend that wasn't long enough, already impatient to get to the next one, thinking about that drink tonight when they finally arrive wherever they're going, worried about catching a cold from the sad sack next to them. If I were to ask this group, "At any time during your high school or your college or even your graduate school years, did you think you would be doing this today?" most of them would say no. But the one who is like me would say, "Hell yes. Even though I'm six clicks deep in the team, I love it."

Personal happiness is important. And how can you be happy in life if you are not happy at work? Since I fell into bizlove, I have been contented all the time—and that certainly isn't who I used to be. In the old days, I would think, Who will pay me for my advice? Now I bestow my advice knowing that it's the giving that matters, not the tangible rewards. In the old days, I used to race for the weekend, I hated my career, I couldn't stand working for The Man. Now, at the end of the day, I feel good about myself. I change people's lives. I love evangelizing others. I have seen them transform. They've become knowledge pack rats, people who are constantly experimenting, learning how to love, saying it aloud.

Bizlove gives you genuine satisfaction.

When you hate your job, you are a zombie. When you love your job, you are alive. To paraphrase Thornton Wilder, bizlove is the bridge between the living and the dead from 8 A.M. to 8 P.M. Some of you are already bright, well-read, and generous with your address books. You are smiling, listening, and touching human beings. In the eyes of your colleagues and partners, you are one of a kind. People search for you to share their opportunities. You have that softly shimmering patina that attracts others like a moth to a lamp. People don't know exactly why, they can't put their finger on it, but the answer is simple. Your killer app is love.

Don't be fooled. Lovecats are not soft and vulnerable. We are glowing, powerful, and respected by our peers. And we are careful about whom we love. Lovecats always love to scale—that is, we make sure our strategies continue to flourish as we love more and more people. After all, the risk of failure affects a great many people in a business setting. If your strategy is about lending money, breaking rules, or showing preferences for specific people, your love won't scale. At some point you run out of money, at some point someone holds you accountable to the rules, at some point the people to whom you've shown preferential treatment haven't rewarded you or your business sufficiently. Your system of giving away these tangibles collapses. You never arrive at a place where you can help a lot of people and sustain your strategy.

This is what I tell those who approach me with cynicism, who ask if it isn't foolish to be generous in business. If you don't keep your guard up, they say, if you give away too much, you'll be eaten alive.

That's not my point, I respond. If I did all those

things, of course my system would collapse. But I am not a dumbcat.

The difference between good and bad love is scale. The question to ask yourself about the love you give is, Does it work if you keep projecting it to a larger group of people? It's not an ethics issue involving when to be nice and when not to be nice. It's a fundamental business issue. When it doesn't make sense to love, don't do it. When it makes sense, do.

Your bizlife and your personal life are different. Personal-life decisions are based on what is best for you, your family, and your friends. Your bizlife decisions are based on that contract you have signed to create more value than your salary reflects. If you don't add value to your team by showing the love toward someone, then don't do it.

✳

So now that you know what a lovecat is, how do you become one? You follow my three steps: You increase your knowledge, you expand your network, and you share your compassion.

I believe that these steps must be followed in order, because by leading with knowledge, you are perceived as wise, which creates credibility for everything else you do. A matchmaker who is wise is one whose connections I most respect. A humanitarian who is wise is one whose hugs I most appreciate.

Leading with knowledge presented me with some of the biggest successes in my bizlife. In fact, it jump-started my career at Yahoo!

When Yahoo! acquired Broadcast.com in 1999, I turned into the prototypical acquisition baby. Acquisition babies need a sponsor if they're to go anywhere in a new company—someone has to say, "This guy is valuable. Pay attention to him." I didn't have a sponsor. I was uncertain of my future.

Speaking at internal breakfast meetings was then part of my job; I enjoyed spinning my people up. I began to do more speaking gigs until one of our regional vice presidents, Mike Nelson, heard me talk at a large Yahoo! conference. Mike decided I had a knack for motivating people.

Yahoo!'s former chief marketing and sales officer, Anil Singh, is one of the brightest minds in the Web business and one cool customer. I felt you needed this man's support in order to become a significant player in the company.

Anil didn't catch every conference presentation. His world is busy. But one day I was giving a speech on the experience economy at a Yahoo! sales conference, and Mike told Anil: "You've got to hear this guy."

The speech went well and my dot.communists loved

it. They were panting to go tear up the world. And as I walked to the back of the room this man of very few words smiled. "That was awesome," Anil said.

Two days later he added me to an executive summit, speaking alongside best-selling author Seth Godin. The feedback there was positive. Jeff Mallet, Yahoo!'s president, then invited me to move from Texas to California and be part of The Team. My career was off and running.

Not long afterward, while working on a deal with Neiman Marcus, I met Ginger Reeder, the company's director of public relations. I immediately began evangelizing her on the idea of network economics through books such as *Net Gain,* and emphasizing customer service as it was being reborn on the Web as described in Patricia Seybold's *Customers.com.* Ginger decided to give me access to Stanley Marcus, chairman emeritus of Neiman Marcus—something she seldom does. But she played matchmaker with no agenda, simply because she thought it was a good idea.

When I met Mr. Stanley (as he is known, to differentiate him from his father, the company's founder), I gained quick credibility by talking about ideas I had learned from my newest book, Sandra Vandermerwe's *Customer Capitalism,* and how they applied to Mr. Stanley. (For more on this book, see pages 104–105.) We also talked at length about Neiman Marcus.

Mr. Stanley told me that if he could change anything, he would turn back the hands of time to the days when the store kept a small box with index cards that salespeople could use to recall every customer's size, favorite colors, and brands. "We've grown too big to do that," he sighed.

But I explained that he could create an equivalent of the card file using the Internet. For example, we talked about Yahoo!'s and Neiman Marcus's new collaboration: We were going to webcast their annual "Big Book" catalog launch, a promotion which invited customers to act as "fantasy gift advisers" so they could suggest the best and most outlandish gifts to place in the catalog, and also sign up for digital updates and printed materials. This would allow Neiman Marcus to listen to their customers and get their permission to talk with them for free, forever. I connected the idea of the Internet with the old corner store in terms of personalization and customized one-to-one service. As Mr. Stanley says, "Consumers are statistics, customers are people."

I also recommended some books and gave him an affectionate hug, and a solid, everlasting connection was sparked.

✳

In the upcoming chapters you will learn how to put bizlove into practice. I believe that everyone can be a lovecat. We all have the necessary pieces inside of us. The rest of it comes from studying, practicing, and perfecting. Think of any human characteristic, such as being observant: We are all born with some degree of observational power, but it can also be learned. And people who need to be observant on the job, from police detectives to card sharks, can sharpen their skills over time.

The same is true for bizlovers. I want you to take whatever qualities you already have that can make you a good lovecat and start honing them to become a great lovecat, beginning with step one: knowledge.

II.

KNOWLEDGE

It's been one of those long, long days. You're sitting at your desk working on a spreadsheet, a report, or a memo. You feel there's nothing left in you. Suddenly you hear the ominous sounds of Big Joe rumbling his way down the hall. You recognize his presence because you can hear all the high-fives, the constant "Hey, man"s, all the phony laughs.

You cringe. If Big Joe tells you he loves you one more time, you're going to lose it.

Love in the context of business has always been more of a communications phenomenon than something of genuine substance. We've tended to associate the idea of office love, with its accompanying hearty hugs and corny expressions, as an attempt to convey affection.

The problem is that such love is often unsubstantiated. Joe doesn't really care for you any more than he cares for the other three dozen people to whom he's just pledged his everlasting affection. In fact, the day he thinks that associating with you will hurt his place on the status ladder, he's gone. Good-bye Joe.

Such people, who say they care for others but who share no real business value, don't sustain themselves for long. No one believes them. Their professions of love waste everyone's time. They are toxic to the workplace.

The fact is, we all need a real foundation to deal with our day-to-day challenges. The word *foundation* makes me think of my Native American relatives, and what they called their *stronghold.* When times were rough, the stronghold was a place where you were always welcome, a place where your family and friends nurtured and defended you.

In today's culture we pick our own strongholds. In business, such places used to be the large corporations, with their clear rules and solid guarantees, their long-term contracts and pension funds. Then, starting in the 1970s, the revolution began—you suddenly became valuable and promotable because of what you knew and not how long you had been there.

Our business stronghold is no longer grounded in a physical workplace. Today it is based in our fellow humans: If you build a stronghold centered on the caring people who support you rather than on the company itself, you'll have something to fall back on if things go awry. Although the rules of business have changed over the years, people haven't.

To create that stronghold, you have to put in some

real work. By that I mean: Accumulate enough knowledge that you can share it with others—so you can enable them to profit from your knowledge as much as you do. A care cocktail can blow up if no attention is paid to the order of its ingredients. Lovecats who hug and kiss without adding value are just like Big Joe—a waste of everyone's time.

*

The first step in cultivating value is to make sure you possess knowledge.

The most common currency at work is social currency, which generally consists of easy conversation: ballgame scores, the weather, fast-breaking gossip. These conversations give everyone an excuse to talk, and if you're able to pass along something that makes others react well, such as the best jokes from last night's talk shows, you've got good social currency. But most of this is inconsequential. Its value passes, as does the value of its purveyor. People conclude, "He's funny, but he's not money."

Knowledge, however, is consequential. Knowledge currency is social currency on steroids. It's important, it's powerful, it's essential. Thus it is *value currency.* Someone talking about the latest reality television show may attract a brief audience around the water cooler or the copy machine, but someone who tells people about Clayton M. Christensen's *Innovator's Dilemma* and who finds a way for them to connect the ideas to their careers so that they own the book (so that they can use it themselves to succeed in their jobs), is a person of genuine value. (*The Innovator's Dilemma* discusses disruptive technologies such as Honda Supercub, Intel's 8088 processor, and hydraulic excavators, and how they helped redefine the competitive landscape of their respective markets.) It's the difference between knowing which sports team is in first place and which new business idea can propel a career forward.

This is why you aggregate wisdom. This is why you transmit knowledge. You're not just handing out some weight-loss hint or a workout tip or a recipe for a great-tasting low-fat cake. You're giving someone the knowledge edge that can advance a career. You're becoming a theory-slinging, expert-quoting, knowledge-throwing lovecat, and that's what makes you stand out from the pack, and that's why others keep calling on you.

Considering how much knowledge is out there to dine on, what do you eat? When you're a student in college, the answer is simple: You anchor your diet around assigned textbooks, you augment your books through additional research, you take notes during your professors' lectures, and you pass a test to prove you did all of the above.

But you're no longer in college. You can do whatever you want. Do you go for variety or do you catch as catch can? Do you try an even mixture—magazines, books, television, and radio? I say there is no option. I've looked at all the possibilities, and for the student of business, books are the answer. Books should be your diet's staple because they are the complete thought-meal, containing hypotheses, data, research, and conclusions, combined in a thorough attempt to transfer knowledge. If they're good, they contain that essential value prop, that meta-idea, or that statement of fact that gives the reader a unique perspective.

Magazine articles are between-meal snacks. They are Ideas Lite. They aren't necessarily intended to transfer entire thoughts, although they may contain a kernel of an idea or some good recommendations for books to read. Now and then you may happen onto some real, powerful knowledge. But those are the exceptions; for the most part, magazine articles are commercial vehicles—publishers use them to position their advertising. They don't build your knowledge stronghold.

The news media—electronic or print—are the equivalent of candy and soda: fun to eat, but hardly appropriate to live on. The ideas expressed in them are too narrow, too transitory, too packaged and predigested for the mass market. In the bizworld, there are few things more potentially embarrassing than trying to make a good point based on what you read in today's paper. Much too often you fail, because the moment you are challenged, your lack of depth becomes readily apparent.

Books give you knowledge. The news gives you awareness. The latter is a measurement of today. Knowledge is a measure of yesterday, today, and tomorrow. Awareness is finite. Knowledge is forever.

We all hear about various 80/20 rules. Twenty percent of the people are responsible for 80 percent of the business, for instance. Or the consultants' favorite selling rule: If you build that million-dollar factory with us, we will build it for $800,000 and do it 20 percent better—i.e., for 80 percent of the original price, you'll get 20 percent bonus value.

Here's another 80/20 rule: Spend 80 percent of your time on books, and 20 percent on articles and newspapers.

And by books, I don't mean just any book. I mean hardcovers. A paperback is made to be read. A hardcover is made to be studied. There's a huge difference. I don't read a book just to say that I've finished it. I read it so that when I'm done, the inside covers are filled with enough notes that I can use this book for as long as I need to.

True, hardcovers are more expensive. But I'm talking about your career. If you can afford to party, or to buy new techno-gadgets, or to eat at fancy restaurants, you can afford a few hardcover books. And if that extra cost makes it a barrier-to-entry for your peers, remember that there are barriers-to-entry in any competitive field. Not only is this one you can easily overcome, but by removing those barriers you give yourself the chance to shine. The books you read today will fuel your earning power tomorrow.

Simply put, hardcover books are the bomb. They are fun to hold. They become personal the first time you mark them up, the first time you bend back the binding. There's something wonderful about the sound of rustling pages. There's something exciting about writing down the ideas that interest you. Soon your book becomes more than just pages between covers. It becomes your ticket to success. Congratulations! You've just achieved traction as a student.

✳

Here's a practical four-step program designed to make knowledge work for you: (1) aggregation, (2) encoding, (3) processing, and (4) application.

Let's talk about step 1, **aggregation.** How do you know which books to read?

When a football coach tells a player he should own the game, he wants him to know more about his position than anyone else on the field. For example, former Dallas Cowboys cornerback Deion Sanders didn't just market himself as Prime Time, he worked like crazy. He watched more videos than anyone else who played his position; he studied wide receivers and quarterbacks on teams he had just played or was about to play, or teams he was watching in other conferences, should they play in the future. Imagine this guy spending hours on end with a stopwatch, timing quarterbacks and receivers, until his knowledge was so great that when the ball was supposed to hit the receiver, instead there was Deion, intercepting it, running it back for a touchdown.

Read books so that you own your own job just like Deion Sanders owned his. If I were that financier who aspires to be a banker, I would want to be fully geeked on the impact of globalism so I could sit comfortably in any meeting, knowing that I could add value to any conversation. Or, if I were that human-relations person who aspires to be the best in her business, I would want to know everything there is to know about human and organizational behavior as it pertained to my job so that I could lead the pack rather than follow. If I acquire the right knowledge, I am actively self-promoting in the best sense of the word; I have been moved up from private to four-star general in others' eyes.

But to aggregate, you must engage in the first step—finding the right material. This is not a difficult process. Bookstores are ubiquitous. Visit them. Wander through the aisles. Be sure you have plenty of time. Look at books carefully. As you do, search for a set of key words that are important to you.

For instance, there are several words or phrases I search out whenever I'm in a bookstore, including *brand marketing, globalism, the new economy, partnerships, strategic alliances, the future.* When I see any of these words in a book's subtitle or on the jacket copy, I pay attention.

I came up with my key words when I first went to Broadcast.com; there I paid attention to every piece of writing that slipped past me, whether on paper or e-mail. And since, like all employees, I had access to the history of the company, I pored over such items as the five biggest proposals we'd made the previous year but didn't win. When certain words kept appearing, such as *brand marketing,* which I knew little about, or *profit-and-loss* accounting, which I didn't understand, I was able to begin shaping my own reading list.

If you are a salesperson, you might look for words such as *negotiation, closing, finding, clients for life, making clients happy, persuasion.* An entrepreneur might seek out *economy theory, macroeconomics, success stories, profit, locating capital, angel investors, raising money, business plans.* A lawyer might look for *negotiation skills, behavioral science, public speaking, the impact of politics on law,* or *the impact of law on politics.*

If you can't come up with specific key words, then stroll through the business section. Pick up as many books as you can. Don't just look at the display piles. Study the spines on the shelves. Read the back covers and the jacket copy. Search out blurbs by other authors whose works you know, or by business leaders whom you admire. Look at the table of contents. Does it interest you? Would knowing its promise help you?

Go online to a bookselling website. There you can type in your key words and research every available volume on the subject. Take advantage of those sites that recommend books. Study which ones people with similar interests purchased and follow the links to them. When you buy from the leaders, like Barnesandnoble.com or Amazon.com, their technology recommends related books each time you revisit the site. How easy is that?

Don't be afraid to buy three to five books at a time. Although this may end up costing you up to a couple of thousand dollars a year, think of it as an investment in your future. That two thousand dollars today could net you many hundreds of thousands of dollars tomorrow.

Be resourceful. Invent ways to lessen the bite. I recently started a trend throughout my friendship circles by convincing their bosses to let them expense-account their business-book purchases, on condition that my friends make them available to other employees at their workplace. Not every boss has agreed, but most of them have, so it's worth a try. You won't hurt your brand by asking.

Next, begin to look for book recommendations in the journals that you're grazing. Magazines such as *Business Week, Business 2.0, Fast Company,* and even the airline magazines will contain excellent recommendations, as well as book reviews and other suggested readings. General newspapers such as *The New York Times* or *USA Today* will also feature books in their daily review columns that may be worth your consideration.

Ask your friends for the titles of their favorite books. Not only will you be able to compile a great list, you present them a way to show you the love. And you'll provide them with an impetus to read more, once they know that their recommendations mean something to others. Even more, buy books for your bizmates. They'll reciprocate. You'll spin it up.

Tip: Hardbacks come covered with dust jackets. Don't take that jacket off. Let the design keep you interested in the book. More important, the colors, the images, and the words will help elicit feedback from others. If you carry around a plain cloth book, few people will ask you what you're reading. If you're holding a book with a flashy jacket, someone will probably wonder about it, giving you the opportunity to share your thoughts and helping you learn to express the book's kernel. You own the theory best when you can fully communicate it to others.

✳

After aggregating, the next step is **encoding**.

Encoding means that you've intelligently and completely digested your knowledge meal.

Before you can properly consume books, however, you have to find places to read, or what I call, in Internet jargon, MyPlaces. Just as you've bookmarked your FavoritePlaces online, do the equivalent with your knowledge diet. Find spots where you like to read, or where you have time to do so. If you're on a plane, a train, or even in a taxi, get used to reading a book. You will begin to associate places where you eat, sleep, travel, and even where you're stuck in traffic with places where you read. Soon you will find that reading becomes second nature whenever you have a spare moment in any of these locales. Unlike computers, books boot up instantly. You should, too. One of my friends recently stopped driving to work so he could take the train and create a one-hour-a-day MyPlace to read.

Not long ago, as I was on my way to Austin to address a group of Dell Computer executives about digital branding, I was reading Phil Carpenter's *eBrands,* a case study of six companies that had built great brands. The moment I saw the plane was stuck on the tarmac, creating one of my key MyPlaces, I read forty pages and marked many passages.

At one point I took a break and saw that the man next to me was staring out into space, and two others across the aisle were reading the in-flight magazine. The odds were excellent that these platinum first-class kind of guys had already read that same magazine twice. Two women near me were fast asleep, while most of the others were on their second drink. Once again I wanted to say: "What the hell are you all doing? Do you realize how fast things are changing? Do you know how close to obsolete you're becoming? Once you may have had a huge lead in life to get where you are today. Why are you going to let people like me catch up with you?"

The easiest place to make a habit of reading is your bed. There you can place any number of books on your night table and dip into one before you go to sleep so it can roll around in your dreams.

Now that you've located the right places to read, you can start encoding.

Keep in mind that you are reading primarily for future application. You aren't doing it for entertainment—although this kind of reading can certainly be enjoyable because when you digest useful information, you look forward to tomorrow, knowing that you are building excellent value currency. Eagerly anticipating your next day at work, especially on a Sunday, can be a remarkable experience. It reminds me of the night before my first day in sixth grade, when I'd laid out my new notebook, new jeans, and a crisp new Dallas Cowboys jersey on the bedroom floor and could hardly sleep. The next day I strutted to school. That's the way I feel today when I am totally prepared to add knowledge value in my business life.

As you read, you must encode: First you *tag*, then you *cliff* the books (a word I invented from reading so many Cliff's Notes while in school).

What this means is: Read actively and interactively. Search your book for something worth retaining, and develop a system that allows you to find that passage again quickly. Always carry a pen—and the smallest one possible, so that you can use it as a bookmark, too. (If you want something fancier, Levenger's catalog sells an elegant book-annotation kit with page points and colored pen-cils.) The point: Always be writing when you're reading.

I tag things by underlining, which forces me to reread the sentence. And I underline slowly, so I am sure to reread carefully. As a child I would watch my mother study her Bible for hours, painstakingly marking it with her pen as she underlined everything she wished to remember. When I asked why she took so long, she told me that she wasn't just underlining—she was studying the passage as she marked it. So that's what I do today. (If the sections are lengthy, or if the book's paper is too porous, clearly marked brackets will work just fine.)

I also make notes in the margins, interpreting the book for future reference. This way, if I don't remember what a difficult section was about, I have my own interpre-tation handy.

When I tag, I look for specific types of content, start-ing with contextual definitions, which are of utmost importance. There are few, if any, dictionary definitions for these words and phrases, so you'll have to depend on books to tell you what they mean. So every time I see a definition, I tag it.

For instance: You can't find a reasonable definition of the phrase "killer app" in the dictionary, and even if you could, the definition probably wouldn't be current. In business, certain words and phrases change their connotation faster than dictionaries are published. If I hadn't tagged and studied the phrase the first time it came up, I would have been quite puzzled the next time I read it.

I had to do the same to harness the tacit meanings of such phrases as "increasing returns," "net present value," and "network effects."

Likewise, if I'm reading a book on management, I might spot good definitions of "metrics," "optimization," or "legacy." The dictionary definitions for such words are often different from those implied by the author, so when they are surrounded by real-world examples, as well as specific explanations based on the word's use in the management field, I tag those, too.

Books also make Big Statements, or passages that explain the kernel of the book with crystal clarity. As a former musician, I liken book kernels to melodies from songs—a small piece of something memorable from a great book that practically sings.

For instance, in *The Tipping Point,* author Malcolm Gladwell uses history and data to show that "ideas and products and messages and behaviors spread just like viruses do." They take on a life of their own and are spread by talented salespeople with unique communications skills.

This idea helps me understand how I can build, control, and leverage social viruses to run my business more efficiently; it also helps me recruit better talent, because now I know a great viral marketer when I see one: I understand the skill set. This gives me an alternative approach to spreading the word about my new products by embracing the swarm and putting them to work marketing for me. That's big.

I also mark statements that are supportive of other kernels in other books. You don't want to be a one-trick pony on major subjects. Once you realize how one book's thesis supports the next, you develop depth. Your depth of knowledge gives you more tools to implement the possibilities in business.

For example, I just finished Emanuel Rosen's *The Anatomy of Buzz*. His Big Thought is that great products spread through buzz and the power of human connectors (great communicators who can pass information to their networks). Since I'd read *The Tipping Point* I was already dialed in to the skills aspect of buzz. I also knew that, historically, when buzz reaches a tipping point, good things start to happen. However, Rosen builds on the idea by noting that buzz marketing can be assisted by the product's packaging and position. Gladwell: Viruses explode. Get talented people who spread the virus and take your idea or product past the tipping point. Rosen: Buzz becomes virus based on person-to-person communication. Gladwell plus Rosen: a complete view of the possibilities of viral/buzz. Double the examples. Depth.

I tag the quotables, or the cool stories, the shining examples, the poetic statements worth citing to bizmates. Kevin Davis provides great salescat-to-salescat advice in his *Getting Into Your Customer's Head.* Here's something I tagged: "The traditional self-focused selling approach is no longer effective because today's new buyers are unwilling to follow you. They don't want to be 'sold.' They want to make educated buying decisions. To make a sale, you must join them on their buying path."

At the same time I tag, I also cliff. Everyone has their own system, and everyone has their own set of abbreviations and notations. Mine is to write notes on the first blank white page inside the book—just a simple one-line summary that helps me reconnect with each of the book's ideas, definitions, and data points when I return to it. Also, the actual act of writing down such notes helps me understand each concept on the spot and makes me more likely to retain it. I write the page number first and then about twenty-five words in my own shorthand. It will take some practice and you'll have to develop abbreviations and readable handwriting, but the exercise will increase your comprehension.

The last part of the cliffing system involves writing down your quotables on the right side of the back cover. It's all future content for presentations in PowerPoint (Microsoft's ubiquitous presentation software) and will greatly help you as you prepare your next speech or writing assignment.

You don't have to copy my system exactly; develop any system that works for you. But develop a system today.

After aggregating and encoding comes **processing**.

Because our college days are behind us, we no longer have teachers, term papers, or final examinations to test how well we've been reading. So we need to make sure we are properly digesting, or processing, all the information we are tagging and cliffing.

As you read a book, depending on its level of complexity, review major sections before you move on. Let's say you're devouring a three-part book on sales management. As you finish section one, go back and review your cliffs to make sure you fully grasp everything you've read before starting section two. This will greatly enrich your understanding of the entire book. Too often we plow ahead,

96: * The greater the Convergence on Biz Model & change. for ABOVE AVG PROFITS
→ THE MODEL MUST BE Unique · PERCEIVED by CustomerS

96: Consanguinity = Big word 4 "FIT" · A Biz Model must
Be internally consistent · all parts pointing to The Same GOAL

97: 4 PROFIT Boosters: ① ↑ Returns ② Barriers ③ Scale ④ Flexibility

100: Positive Feedback Effect · take early lead · rule is winner take all · Overwhelm

102: Barriers Created Thru ① Pre-Emption ② Choke Points ③ Cust Lock In

103: 1st Mover is compelling w/ ① Rapid Tech change ② Short Prod Line Cycle
→ Pre-emption = ① Absorb Head ② Capacity Z Leapfrost ③ Willing to Double bets (R&D)

105: CHOKE POINT = owning uniquely · Assets, Interface, Standard, Infrastructure
→ Can you leverage such ownership to charge a toll

108: FRAGMENTED industries = good fodder for Consolidation & Scale effects/Advs
→ Strategic Economies & driven by ① Scale ② Focus ③ Scope

109: Scale Economies · Come from sharing "costs" Across Biz Units / Divisions

102: Look FOR Things where The Rate of Change is Changing (Discontinuities)
→ Rates of change between diff Phenom ultimately Converge → Fast Eats Slow!
When Society Changes Taste then The Market · differentials = opportunity

126: In industries, we're blind in The Same ways: We pay Attn to Same Things & ignore Same Things
→ The key is to notice Things That the Rest of the Industry is ignoring

129: Look @ trends That ① are large ② impact You · 2nd Largest bet: "Bet The " "And The x what happens"

134: If U come up w/ A set of questions RE · "Unfamiliar" → you'll take away valuable insight

136: BizModel = "Thing". Mental Model = Attributes about The Thing.

150: Political Model = Def how power is distributed Throughout an Org/Biz 12
→ Power to Enforce Mental Models → operation · Biz-Model · Political Models

173: Playstation II · Kutaragi · SUMO Ring = · doh you

188: An activist's point of View · Change · Opportunities · Bus Concepts Z Exploit
→ Point of View must be: CREDIBLE · COHERENT · COMPELLING · COMMERCIAL

192: Data Bombs: Explode while reading · Builds Hi Impact Inductive Case

197: Gatekeepers & bi-level events = STRATEGIC INFECTION POINTS

232: Cisco: If we don't MAKE it EZ for Customers Z Replace our technology
WITH NEW TECHNOLOGIES, our Customers will do it 4 us

246: Too MANY Companies define Themselves Based on what They do
NOT what They know — AND What They own

247: GE Welch: Redefine Biz where your MKTShare is only 10%

248: Worth in an Organization is Based on what Somebody Knows

252: The Capacity for Radical Innov ↑ Proportionately w/ every mile away from HQ

254: Silicon Valley = 3 Things: Valley of ① Ideas ② Talent ③ CAPITAL

262: What matters is New Econ & ROI: Its Return On Imagination ④

263/264: Old School = Resource Allocation · New School = Resource Attraction

261: In early Stages of New Biz Concept U should maximize the Ratio of learning over investment.
→ GE Bubbles = Units That make $254 Third per year

271: Size of Biz ≠ Issue: Orthodoxy Z single Biz Model = Issue/Threat

285: WCI — Wealth Creation Index → 107 Billion Retail Surrendered
to Startups 88-2000

296: U can't keep up w/ innovation Unless Customers = Co-Developers

xi: Its Not Old vs New Econ: Its innovators vs. non-innov (capacity)
→ its the power of I (innov) Not E that Separates Winners in 21st C

10: The Barbarians aren't banging on the gate, they're eating off your best china
→ For the 1st time we can work backwards from imagined rather than forward from our past ✳

2: One CEO focused on How we did it. Now focus on WHAT we will do!
→ By the time U wring out the last 5% of How, there is a new WHAT

3: KNOWLEDGE is now COMMODITY — you can Buy it by the Pound! → LKA
5: Ind Revolutionaries take Big Concept. Not Prod/Service as start point
6: Devise stuff oreo of Bizcon. Innov its linear "improve" innovation
3: Biz Concept Innov = The corpet Ado in The Age of Revolution
→ Def: New Biz Model = 1) New Cost value 2) Surprise & Compet 3) wealth & investors
→ Revolutionaries don't Release wealth. They Build it. Don't Conserve - CREATE
0: having planners create strategy is like Bricklayers doing Michelangelo
4: Activists Roles: Marsella - Gandhi - King et al - found that they attempted peace
6: EMERSON: 2 Parties - always - The Estab & THE MOVEMENT
4-27. Innov Regimes: 1900-1950 Science 50-90s: Brand Mkt Now: Biz Concept
53: Sooner or later every Biz Model Reaches & Returns that's happening some day later
    Rule taker or Rule maker/Rule breaker
54: Dakota Tribal Wisdom: When U R on a dead horse best strategy is 2 Dismount
57: U know U have problems when D.C. pays more Attn to your Cust than U do!
→ In the age of Revolution C's must - Opp Seeking Missiles Possibilities or the Accomplishments
9: Big Truth: What is NOT DIFFERENT is NOT STRATEGIC
8: Biz Model breakout: Interface | Strat | Resources | Value net →
4: Efficient: ValveCust assign 2 Benefits — Cost of delivering Benefits
                    Benefits   Config   Boundaries
7: Bizconcept Innov = The search for Temporary monopolies — Benefit V / Benefit C
→ This Drives 1) Returns & Compet lock out
8: Revolutionary goal of Strategy is to Create imperfect Competition
2: When U See a Window of Opp - Crawl Thru it & lock the door behind U
09: Lack of Bizfocus: = Trying to "Boil The Ocean"
111: Some Biz Models R easier to Re-Config than Others. They will survive Revolution
20: Companies Fail 2 Predict the future not Because they can't predict it - Cuz they can't Imagine it
    → its vitally import to know difference tween "The Future" & "The Imagined"
    You can't be Rev a/o Revol point of view don't hire a guru - Be your own guru
21: PERSPECTIVE IS WORTH 80 IQ Points - Vision over Brainpower
→ Each Revol of Art was driven by new concepts of Reality
28: WILLIAM GIBSON - The Future has already happened - Its Just Unequally distributed!
35: In the age of Revolution - The Future I more of the past - Its different Than the past
37: The problem w/ the future & its unknowable; it is DIFFERENT
4: The Organ Isn't "Them" - Its U. Stop whining about "them"
17: ENRON: THERE'S No Biz that can't be Restructured & Revolutionized
147: Virgin Biz Dev Rules: 1)Challenge 2)Give Cust freedks 3)Entertain/Fun
154: Silicon Valley = Refugee Camp for Revolutionaries That could get a Tre... elsewhere
280: Industry Revolutionaries are a missile up the Tailpipe. Boom! You're irrelevant
195: Capital Intensive vs imagination intensive innovation

my copy of Gary Hamel's *Leading the Revolution* (Boston, Massachusetts: Harvard Business School Press, 2000).

unsure of ourselves but too impatient to turn back. Instead, review. We always did in school—because it works.

Whenever you have a reading session that lasts longer than thirty minutes (which in my experience is approximately as much time as most people will concentrate on something new), close the book and your eyes. Let your mind drift for a few minutes. Allow ideas to connect in your head in ways that won't happen on paper.

Once you've finished the book, write a review. Do it as a summary for yourself, or log on to one of the online bookstores, where you can post your review for others to read. People will rate it, respond to it, and read your profile; maybe you'll find an affinity with a group of people and create a digital book club.

The review doesn't have to be lengthy. Just describe the book's Big Thought, how well the author conveyed that thought, and how valuable you feel the idea is. You might pass along your favorite quote, too.

Join or form a real-life book club. If you don't have enough friends who read, try a local bookstore or see if you can create a reading group at work. Send e-mails to coworkers and suggest you meet once a month in the cafeteria to discuss a new book. Be original. Melissa Goidel, one of Yahoo!'s rising stars, asks her staff to create a list of thirty to forty books they think are important. Every month each of the six reads a different book and reports on it to the others. This way they all learn the essence of seventy-two new books a year.

Vary the style of books you read. I often find myself locked in to upscale business books from a Major Business School Press. Sometimes you have to read outside that box. A few years ago I tried *The Art of Happiness* by the Dalai Lama and *Toward a Psychology of Being* by Abraham Maslow to get a different sort of expert view into human motivation; both books expanded my lovecat abilities.

The Dalai Lama helped me as a manager, teaching me about the ethics of human relationships, in and out of business. And he took the weight of the world off my shoulders, because he said, "You don't have to be a god. Just stop hurting people." Strangely enough, I didn't know that—I'd thought you had to fix the impossible on a daily basis. He also taught me that you can't be good to all people all the time, but by practicing patience and tolerance, you can stop being bad to people, which was important for me vis-à-vis my feelings about employees and competitors.

Reading Maslow is like putting on a new pair of glasses that allow you to see people more clearly. He says, "Although human beings are capable of being selfish, lustful, and aggressive, that is not what they are fundamentally. Beneath the surface, at the psychological and biological core of human nature, we find basic goodness and decency. When people appear to be something other than good and decent, it is only because they are reacting to stress, pain, or the deprivation of basic human needs such as security, love, and self-esteem."

I was already aware that businesspeople were suspicious of others, and with good reason, considering the occasional betrayal and duplicity. But Maslow taught me that people are good unless proven otherwise, and when they are bad, it's because they are coping with some need beyond their control.

If you understand the difference between human nature and motivation, you can better predict human interactions, you can explain away aberrations, and you will become more rational about people, making you a better manager, helping you become a lovecat.

Borrow other people's books to see how they have tagged and cliffed them, and you'll also gain a new perspective. I've started doing this more and more; seeing how someone else perceives a book often gives me an entirely new understanding. We then talk about our book-reading techniques and together we build a better knowledge mousetrap.

But never borrow the book as a substitute for owning and studying it yourself—you don't want to miss the marking process. If you can stomach the metaphor, merely scanning another person's notes without actually reading the text is a little like digesting someone else's meal.

A few more notes on processing: Make a commitment to review as many as one or two books a week. But when you review, it's not necessary to reread the entire book. Go back to a book that has some relevance to a new project, a new discussion, or a new dream, and look over your cliffs in the front of the book. If you've done a good job cliffing, it shouldn't take you more than half an hour to recall the book's message. Then close your eyes and let your mind roam over the subject.

If you do this regularly, the books you are currently reading will make more sense, especially when they relate to your old favorites. For example, I'm currently reading a book on business innovation called *Leading the Revolution,* by Gary Hamel. Hamel argues that innovation is more important than invention—and that true innovation means demolishing and re-creating an entire business concept. Along the way, he discusses how IBM completely innovated itself into a new kind of business (transforming itself from a product company to a service company), and how Starbucks innovated a business from scratch. To build up to his Big Thought, Hamel uses little ideas that are supported by other books I have already read, and these subconcepts jog my memory. So as I read through his idea that the value of your network is the square of the number of people in it, I think about John Hagel's *Net Gain,* because that's the premise of his book—grow your network and you become value squared. By understanding Hamel, I more fully understand Hagel.

Occasionally you may find magazine articles that validate or negate theories in your library of digested books. Tear out the article and slide it inside the relevant book for future reference. Annotate the article before storing it in the book, so you can easily remember its significance later. Some of my books end up looking like small filing cabinets.

Take your finished books to work and create a library. Because they'll surround you all day long, you are much more likely to share ideas in them with your bizpartners than if you kept them at home.

I have two personal libraries. One stays at home, and consists of books I haven't yet read, and the other, at my office, includes completely read and digested books. The workplace library makes it easy for me to refer to books while doing business and allows me to be more productive with my downtime. My library is a wonderful conversation starter, and I'm constantly relying on it during my never-ending efforts to recruit new lovecats.

Note: Stock your library with extra copies of your favorite books. It's hard to beat the gift of a book, especially right after a meeting.

After aggregating, encoding, and processing comes the last step, **application,** which is really about sharing. Just as the reason we own things is to share them with others, the reason we acquire knowledge is to share it. Otherwise, we don't truly distribute love.

Application is the employment and leverage of your knowledge in the workplace. For instance, let's say you're in the printing business and you're talking to your peers about a book on the digital economy and its implications for your clients. You convey the kernel of that idea in such a concise way that your peers can now look at their business through new eyes; or, better, you get them so stoked that they go out and purchase the book themselves. Or you buy them the book yourself—that's the ultimate act of application.

Too many people internalize their new information, turning it into private wisdom that cools in their intellectual cellar. Their wisdom gains no distribution. This is a little like producing a great cable-access show that never reaches a public audience.

The best part of sharing knowledge: The more you

apply it, the more you get in return. Knowledge gives you insight, which makes your bizlife easier and leads you to better strategies and clearer vision. You create a positive feedback loop. Some of the most potent knowledge in my arsenal comes from people who've turned me on to a book that I never would have found if I hadn't been evangelizing one of my favorite books to them.

A final advantage of application: When you talk about a book, it forces you to know it inside and out. The other night I had dinner with Oren Aviv, the president of marketing at Disney's Buena Vista Motion Pictures. I'd just finished reading *Building Brandwidth,* by Sergio Zyman and Scott Miller, which argues that marketing is comprised of everything a company does, from how its product is packaged to how it is positioned in the eyes of the consumer through advertising and promotion. All these things define the benefit to the user. If you have created a good product and packaged it well, you deliver on the promise. You then create anticipation on the part of the consumer.

For example, Heinz repeatedly tells us through their packaging, advertising, and copy that their ketchup ("It's making me wait") is so thick and delicious that our mouths start to water while we wait for it to ooze out of the bottle onto our French fries. It's the power (and value) of suggestion.

Likewise, I told Oren, every way Disney packages a

video game or edits a Disney movie trailer must add value to consumers when they buy or use the product. It must make the consumer eagerly anticipate the Disney experience. Oren agreed, adding that this gave him a fresh and affirming perspective: From now on, whenever he looked at an advertisement, instead of wondering if it was entertaining or funny, he'd ask if it added value to the transaction. If it didn't, it wouldn't fly.

When I returned to the office, I sent him the book so he could own the idea himself.

When considering application, think about how you will apply what you have read to your peers and partners. You are building your brand, so when these people think about you, they think about the knowledge you have passed on to them. And you do that by adding or multiplying value in conversation based on what you now know. You are going to try to use theories, suggestions, and research from books to solve business problems—after all, many day-to-day business problems are avoidable or solvable with theory. That's why M.B.A.'s exist. In the game of life, they're the ones who are reading from the top of the game box, where the rules are written.

Recently I spoke to a Washington, D.C.–based B2B start-up company called Equal Footing, an auction site for businesses. At 9 P.M. they were still hard at work, as they had been since six that morning. They thought we were going to sit down and summarily review their marketing strategies. But I was trying to find a way to stoke and elevate the conversation, so I told them about a book called *Race for the World,* by Lowell L. Bryan, Jeremy Oppenheim, Wilhelm Rall, and Jane Fraser.

Knowing the book would give the Equal Footing partners a unique perspective as they grew their business, I grabbed a Magic Marker and drew (as best I could) a graphic representation of the book's Big Thought (which turned out to look like a series of circles representing the legacy leaders of today, with a circle at the top representing the nimble little company that would own all the big circles later). Companies that nurture their intangibles (their reputation, talent, and knowledge) rather than their tangibles (their physical plant, their hardware) will emerge in the new world as shapers. These companies will shape the market while the others will become reactors.

Race for the World represented practical, good news to Equal Footing, and I was the first person to apply this valuable social currency to their current business context. Angie Kim, the company's president, wrote me a note the next day thanking me for the ideas that the meeting inspired. That's the payoff with knowledge as social currency. It leads to ideas, solutions, and strong relationships.

Note: The earlier you learn and evangelize a book, the more you will profit from it. And you'll have the opportunity to be among the first to ascend that steep learning curve, which means that you'll know more rapidly when a new idea is relevant to business. While others are still figuring it out, you've become the authority. So don't wait until a book hits the best-seller list to pick it up. Experiment on your own. Listen to friends; if someone gives you a good book early on, let him or her know how much you appreciate the gesture so that you maintain the connection. And develop a strong relationship with your local booksellers so they will guide you to books similar to ones you've already bought.

✳

Application entails four steps, as well as some additional notes for the communications-challenged. These steps are all interconnected. Each step leads to the next.

Step 1: Make sure that you own the book's Big Thought, which results from your encoding and processing.

When you know the idea well, try to draw it as I did for the people at Equal Footing with *Race for the World*. You don't have to be Picasso, but there's something about watching a friend sketch out a sequence of business events that helps create real understanding. Ever notice how the paper tablecloths at restaurants end up covered with all kinds of schematic diagrams? And what are those doodles? Usually awkwardly drawn designs of a new idea, a new plan, or a new business.

Step 2: Visualize a discussion.

This may seem difficult when you first start, but eventually it will feel quite natural.

When you're done with a book, close your eyes and summarize the Big Thought in your mind. Review scenes from your bizlife in which you could use this idea. These scenes will render some of your best Costanza Moments. Remember George Costanza, the quintessentially neurotic sidekick on the TV show *Seinfeld*? Once, after a coworker insulted him, George didn't know how to respond, so for the next several days he drove around in his car, thinking about what he should have and would have and could have said.

We've all had these Costanza Moments when we sat around like a bump on a log during an important discussion and didn't add to the conversation—and then wished we had. Maybe someone was talking about their fear of change, and you didn't know how to contribute. But if you'd read Spencer Johnson's *Who Moved My Cheese?*, you could have related the allegory that would help her understand that change is necessary. Maybe someone was worried about job turnover and volatility; if you'd known Dale Carnegie's *How to Win Friends and Influence People*, you could have recommended it for advice on how to be likable even in troubled times. If someone expressed confusion on how to deal with customers, and you'd read *Built to Last* by James C. Collins and Jerry I. Porras, you could have explained how to build a company with long-lasting value through loyal customer satisfaction. And someone looking for new trends and behavior patterns in the e-commerce sector might profit from *Why People Buy*, by Paco Underhill, which clarifies the mentality of shoppers.

Also, when you've finished a book, search your imagination for scenes from work where you could have added value by bringing up the Big Thought. Review these scenes until you have found three.

Next, imagine which of your friends would appreciate the idea. Instead of dreaming up specific situations where you could have added value, think about specific people who would appreciate your new knowledge. This isn't much different from those times when, as teenagers, we bought great records and couldn't wait to play them for our best friends because we knew they would dig them—

when their eyes lit up, it made us feel like deejays. Here you can be an idea deejay.

Think about your new acquaintances and contacts. True, we don't all have a continual stream of new people running through our lives, but the average person meets, electronically and physically, five times more people in a year than our parents did in similar job functions. Imagine which of your new contacts would appreciate your new social currency. Instead of talking about the weather or sports, share ideas.

I keep a list of books in my head next to my great set of political jokes and sports predictions, all ammo for conversations with new contacts. Rather than the weather, this should be the first bullet in your gun.

For instance, the next time I meet another dude from Texas Instruments on the train to work (I've met five already this year), I'll be ready to talk about Ray Kurzweil's *The Age of Spiritual Machines,* which focuses on artificial intelligence—he says that in twenty years, the standard thousand-dollar computer will match the power of the human brain. When the Texas Instruments guys wonder how techies will remain relevant, I've got an answer, with quotes and perspective to follow. I am already visualizing the conversation, all prepped like a quarterback waiting for my first play. I just need a completion.

Step 3: Look for insert points.

Remember when you were a kid and came home one day to find your parents weren't around and the front door was locked? What did you do? You broke into your own house. You did it by carefully walking around the house until you found a place where you could squeeze inside. Maybe the back door was open, or a bedroom window was ajar, or there was a secret entrance only you knew about—all insert points, some as conspicuous as the front door, some as subtle as an unlocked window.

The same goes for conversation. If you pay attention, you will find insert points that enable you to add value. Maybe it won't come to you like an open door. You may not be so lucky as to have someone say, "Read any good books lately?" But in conversations people convey everything from problems to questions to worries. That's the social currency that most people share.

"Hey, Sara, how are you doing?" I say.

"I'm hanging in there," she responds. But after we break into a deeper conversation, she confesses that as the only female executive at her company, she often feels left out. She can't find her way and she feels that the men around her are somehow speaking a different language than she is.

"Really?" I ask. "Have you read Gail Evans's *Play Like a Man, Win Like a Woman*? She's an executive veep at CNN—she's seen it all and she'll tell you all those male rules of business you totally need to know about, like when to take a risk, or how to play on a team."

I find that whenever someone shares their problems with me, I listen for insert points that would allow me to pass along a Big Thought that might offer a little clarity, or just some perspective. Sometimes the effect of a Big Thought isn't so much that it provides a solution, but that it gives us a new way of seeing the world. It's a fresh perspective. Alan Kay, father of the personal computer, says that perspective is worth fifty IQ points.

The moment an insert point presents itself, I open my mouth and attempt what I call an Elevator Speech—or, what you would say if you were on an elevator with an important bizcontact and had three floors to describe a new concept. (Five years ago, if you were trying to start a new company in Silicon Valley, you had to have a speedy Elevator Speech ready or you couldn't get money. Buildings here aren't very tall.) Most people's attention span is short—even if you have a great solution to their problem, they'll lose interest if it takes you too long to articulate it.

After you've explained the Big Thought, solicit feedback. Ask what others think. Let them talk. The more they're involved in the conversation, the more they'll enter your circle. Then follow up. It's easy to do with e-mail. Tell them you enjoyed the conversation. E-mail a link to the book's catalog page on an online retailer to facilitate their purchase. Or send them the book itself.

Allow for mistakes. Sometimes you may feel you've picked the wrong insert point, or you can't describe the book as well as you expected to. Don't worry. Even a stumbled attempt is more valuable than a rant about the weather or an analysis of last night's reality TV show. The more you practice, the more you'll get it right. But that doesn't mean that accomplished lovecats won't make mistakes. We all do, all the time. That's just part of being human.

And now a special note for the communications-challenged, those of you who read a book and then say to yourself, "I can't communicate this idea to anyone. I'm just not a talker."

Here's some help. Look for insert points that can occur in writing instead of in conversation. Many of us who don't like to talk, like to write. We communicate through memos, e-mail, and faxes. (The truly communications-averse even use voice mail after hours when they know no one will pick up the phone.)

When you write out your ideas, or give a prepared summary, you can practice it until you perfect it. And the feedback is staggered; because it happens over time, you needn't be anxious about responding immediately. If you start by writing, positive feedback will give you the confidence to speak aloud—which is what this is all about.

Go back to the visualization process and this time write a letter about a book you've read. Then select five people from across your network span: workplace, customers, partners (but avoid your boss at this point, since we want a quick win—we don't want to be smacked down from above). Add a friend or two. E-mail these five people your note. Now you're beginning a conversation. Within two communications, make it your goal to talk on the phone or in person about the idea.

Don't stay hidden behind written communication too long. Discussion is about human feedback, about measuring those friendly eyes and those excited smiles that let you know what a difference you are making.

Step 4: Play doctor.

When we were kids, we loved to role-play, and doctor was one of our best roles. Try it again today. Prescribe books to contacts like a doctor would prescribe medications to patients.

For example, let's say you work in marketing at a large

consumer company. I've decided that I truly want you to succeed. So I show you love. I take a look at your role, your aspirations, and your challenges. If I know something based on my experience and my reading, I will share that with you, and help you to own it yourself.

In other words, I won't just tell you about an idea; I will tell you who said it, in what context, and why. To top it off, I might send you the book itself, so you know as much as I do in as short a period of time as possible.

Let's say you tell me that you're having a hard time in Europe competing against your major rival. Your products don't stand out. First, I ask you about your problems. "Is your company strategy leading with packaging, or are you leading with positioning?" Then I discuss the change in the new culture where positioning becomes more important than packaging, relying on Jack Trout and Steve Rivkin's *Differentiate or Die* for my perspective and expertise. Then I prescribe the book for you, so that you can soon own their ideas yourself.

Or let's say you're a stockbroker, but you aspire to be an investment banker; in the meantime, you are making those difficult cold calls to pick up initial accounts. I would prescribe a book about global economic theory. That will be important as you help your clients understand the broader picture of the markets. It's the difference between a broker who offers conventional wisdom and a broker who can make you smarter. Or maybe I would tell you to read about the impact of technology on economics, from biotech to high tech. This might help not only your customers, but also your boss or the finance manager down the hall.

I recently participated in some meetings between Yahoo! and Compaq computers, where I met with Gary Elliot, Compaq's vice president of worldwide integrated marketing communications. These negotiations were arduous and I had genuine compassion for Gary. So early on I launched into the full-court lovecat gig. I went into positive reinforcement mode (smiling at Gary when he had a stressful day and needed some relief). I lent him my address book when he wanted relevant contacts inside our company. I made sure I was the friendly eyes in the meeting, so that whenever Gary looked our way, someone was smiling at him. I shook his hand firmly, I walked him to the elevator, I thanked him for coming.

During our conversations I discovered Gary was focused on, and was a student of, Hewlett-Packard, his major competitor. I shared with him my belief that HP's recent success was due in part to having understood the concept behind Sandra Vandermerwe's *Customer Capitalism.*

Sandra's Big Thought: If you are a company that sells products, you must understand that your customers are in a "customer activity space," or, a mode of doing many things around some activity. They're not just buying a product; they're buying and thinking about many choices, so you have to surround all those choices with your company, or you'll lose them.

For example: You may think of FedEx only for its overnight delivery, but what made them successful was their comprehensive logistics management, allowing your company to track everything that leaves your door and arrives at the recipient's. So before you ever send a thing, you can go to FedEx's website, buy their materials, find out about costs and timing, study the insurance plans, learn how to track packages online. After the package has been delivered, you are offered a historical look at all the logistics you need to manage your budget in the future, as well as to anticipate storage or delivery issues. So instead of just offering a delivery service like their competitors, FedEx surrounds the activity space of logistics management, providing a total solution before, during, and after the actual package is sent. This keeps competitors out and customers in.

HP had configured its market strategy around this

same perspective; they weren't just selling computers, they were surrounding their entire customer-activity space with managing information and knowledge. If you're a company, you don't buy computers to run a website or run a database per se, you buy them to manage information. HP had developed product offerings for every step of the way toward that goal. You need new gear for bandwidth? They've got it. You need new software? They've got it. You need personal service to install it all? They've got it.

I could tell that Gary was intrigued by my description of the book. By the time he had left the meeting room and arrived in our lobby, I was back in my cubicle buying the book online and sending it to him with a note telling him to read chapter eight, where he'd find the essence of my point. Ever since then, I've noticed a new warmth in Gary's e-mails. Not long ago he sent me *The Profit Zone,* by Adrian Slywotzky, David J. Morrison, and Bob Andelman, on how to unlock value in profit. This book will be important to me because it clarifies how to recognize which part of a company is most likely to make money, a valuable skill over time.

Another note, this time for the completely communications-challenged: If the above still frightens you, try joining online communities. Search the bulletin boards on the Web by subject group. Look for e-mail discussion groups in which messages are automatically sent to you. Join one that relates to what you have decided to read.

And a hint for the communications-gifted: Create your own opportunities by being conspicuous. Don't make all your MyPlaces private ones. Read while taking a train, while eating, while taking a break—public situations that can inspire that magic question: "What's that you're reading?" That's the biggest, fattest, largest insert point that will ever hit you over the head.

Note: If you haven't found some application within a few months of reading your books, question your aggregation methods. I try to use a new book as soon as possible with my peers or friends so I can assess its immediate value currency. This isn't always the reality, but it's always the aspiration.

If you're not using the books in your conversation and your business strategy, review your selection process. One easy trick in a bookstore: Open a book and glance at the table of contents. Study the blurbs. Sit down and read the most interesting chapter. Be imaginative. What if you knew everything the author said? What if it was knowledge you could use in the upcoming week? Where would it be useful? Who would you want to spread the new weed to?

Sometimes you will find a home for a book that's

ahead of the curve—one that's not useful now but will be in a year. Most of what you read, however, you'll want to apply fairly quickly. If that's not happening, think about the questions you have asked yourself. What do you really want to do? Maybe your goals have changed and you're reading books that aren't in line with your aspirations. Or maybe you haven't been honest with yourself and although you're thinking that you want to be upper management, none of the issues involved actually interests you. Maybe your job has been changing, and you haven't been tracking it carefully, so that the books you're reading on finance aren't really applicable to your new, more management-oriented tasks.

Go back to your first shopping list and rethink your choices as honestly as possible. Your failure to pick up applicable knowledge may be a sign: Perhaps your aspirations don't jibe with your job.

When the application is right, you'll know it. For instance, a few years ago a friend, Chris Flannery, was working for Westmarine, the largest marine retailer in the world, where he was asked to help restrategize the company. The CFO, John Zott, knew Chris was foundering and recommended a book on project management called *Making It Happen,* by Mackenzie Kyle. "The book explained in plain English how to manage a project, with particular emphasis on human interaction and simple skills," Chris says. It was the key to his success, and he has since lent it to countless others.

By the way, when you feel strongly about a book, write a fan letter to the author. Fifteen years ago Steve Leveen, whom I first met at a 1999 roundtable discussion, founded the successful catalog company Levenger with his wife, Lori. Shortly afterward a sales rep told him to read a book called *Minding the Store* by my new contact Stanley Marcus. "It changed my life," Steve says. "It helped me find my calling as a merchant. It showed me that being a merchant could be a noble thing, something more than just selling stuff to people."

Steve wrote Mr. Stanley a letter and received a response that set in motion a correspondence that has continued for many years and has helped Steve enormously. Mr. Stanley encouraged Steve to join the Young Presidents Organization, which he did, and which has had a tremendous impact on his career. And he has given Steve specific information on retailing. "Mr. Stanley told me that one of the ways great merchants are differentiated from the not-so-great ones is: Don't go just by how much the product sells. Decide if the product is right for your customers. If it isn't, even if it's selling well, it could be wrong for your company and hinder your ability to build a loyal brand. It's not just about making money. It's about knowing your customers and selling them what is good and right for them."

At one point the Levenger company designed some T-shirts and sweatshirts to be sold in their catalog. According to Steve, "Mr. Stanley called and said, 'I don't care how many T-shirts you sell, they don't belong in your catalog.' He was right. Levenger is about tools for readers, not clothes. We got out before we made too big a mistake."

The ability to transfer knowledge is a huge advantage for anyone struggling to succeed in the new economy. It's an easy skill to learn, it's simple to facilitate, and there are more good books than you will ever be able to use, which means that the resources are unlimited. In fact, it's so easy, there's no reason why you shouldn't start now. Buy a book. Carry it with you. Its power is so great that you will feel as though you were carrying plutonium in a briefcase. A well-read lovecat is a lion in the jungle, not a tabby. Roar on.

III.

NETWORK

Remember the old *I Love Lucy* episode where Lucy decides that one of her single girlfriends should be fixed up with a nice single man? So when husband Ricky's male friend comes to New York, Lucy arranges a meeting. Except, of course, everything goes wrong—the female friend cancels out on the date, the man thinks Lucy is really after him, and in the end Lucy is lectured for her silly, meddling ways. Interfering with other people's lives, Ricky tells her, is a no-no.

Poor Lucy. But she's not alone. Our culture is filled with images of matchmakers as bumblers, busybodies, or just plain dunces. In movies, books, even cartoons, matchmakers are never the heroes, always the also-rans. And it's true for real life, too, where romantic matchmaking efforts never seem to pan out. It's difficult to find that one special person for someone else. And the matchmaker gets the blame. There you are, counting the minutes on a miserable date, forever branding the matchmaker as the idiot who created this awkward situation.

But being a business matchmaker is a completely different matter.

Let's say your best friend has been exiled to a desert island (movies come up with premises like this, so why can't I?). His only hope of ever finding a mate lies with you. Once a month you bring him someone to meet. Your stranded friend will react very differently from your pals who aren't stuck on islands. He's thrilled to meet anyone. He has no other options. So if the matchmaking doesn't work out, he's still better off than he was before. At least he has someone new to talk to.

The rest of us, with all our social resources, don't feel as hopeless. We tend to be much more critical of whoever comes our way. ("What the hell were you thinking when you fixed me up with that psycho?" we ask indignantly.)

Today's work world resembles a desert island. The new economy has taken this business continent we've grown to know so well over the last century and blown it apart into what seems like a billion pieces, sometimes making our careers feel as lonely as a remote spot in the ocean, with no one to share our feelings or give us support when we need it.

If you travel often enough to know those forlorn 8 A.M. flights to Chicago or San Diego or Boston, you know that faraway look in people's eyes as they board their eighth airplane that month. You know they're on their own little island. Their only hope is that someone will bring a friend over to their deserted corner of the world. What else can they say but "Thanks for thinking of me"?

Furthermore, back in the realm of personal relationships, you're not really sure who's right for whom because the rules are so complex. It's hard to know what motivates people to make intimate connections—in fact, they often don't know themselves. The wealth of data is missing. It's not about annual reports, the bottom line, or sales growth. It's about chemistry, and no one in history has been able to explain that.

In business, however, you have a much better idea as to whether the introduction you have in mind will add value. Business models are more straightforward—bizpeople tend to know what they are looking for going into any situation. Common necessities and adjacent resources aren't difficult to align. So when you're lining up a connection in the business sense, you're facing a clearly stated need.

While we collect marbles, baseball cards, and antiques in order to hold on to them while they increase in value, the purpose of collecting contacts is to give them away—to match them with other contacts. Whenever you introduce people, instead of one plus one equaling two, it equals two to infinity—because when we make a successful connection, we are helping create that one-in-a-million business relationship with which we are forever associated and that may connect us to myriad new network nodes.

Forget about the personal-world stereotypes. Matchmaking in the bizworld carries a significantly lower risk, because bizpeople must always grow their networks. We constantly need employees, investors, partners, suppliers, peers, strategic alliances, well-wishers, and more. We have to keep current with trends, keep track of our competitors, and keep up with the Big Thoughts that drive our industries. After all, if you have a Big Thought, such as building a huge database of addresses for a catalog business, you'll need to know if postage costs are about to rise or if printing prices are poised to change. Other people's information will affect the truth of your Big Thought, and fast. Yesterday's Big Thought can be today's Big Blunder. Sometimes the people in your network are the only ones who can let you know that.

Eventually, all the people to whom you've connected yourself become, essentially, maintenance-free reserves. Just as we keep extra coal for cold winters or extra money for tough times, these contacts lie in wait, all of them with the potential to repair a looming crisis or add value to a limited opportunity. And even though you don't exact a fixed price for putting them in your network, they may well feel that they'd like to do something for you in return.

These reserves can also be critical for success. Think about business you have lost, or promotions someone else grabbed, or competitive one-on-one situations where a rival triumphed. Calculate the size of the winner's network versus yours. For the most part, the winners are those with the largest networks, the most powerful connections, and the ability to call in their reserves at the moment of truth.

The nodes in your network can accomplish almost anything for you. They can help you find your next job. How many times have you heard people say that they found their job only because a friend told them about it? Your contacts can enlighten you. Almost everyone in my network is a knowledge-transfer agent; they pass along book recommendations, they tell me which new people I should seek out and meet, they inform me of concepts I need to know.

These people are also confidence builders. Remember when, as a teenager, you went to a party where you knew everyone—think about the assurance that gave you. Now remember a party where you knew no one in a sea of a hundred strangers. Your chances of having a good time in that situation were small. Business is no different. The more people you know and, specifically, the more people who have already had positive dealings with you, the more confidence you'll have as you spin your web out farther and farther.

One of the New Big Things in the world of information technology is the concept that software can automate person-to-person business relationships. Consider one of the world's fastest-growing companies, Siebel Systems, which makes a product called Sales Force Automation (SFA) for customer-relationship management. Siebel understands—just as you must—that this is the new form of strategic asset management. Relationships in business are assets to be organized, managed, cultivated, and leveraged, just like capital or cash-on-hand. These SFA products have become so popular that half of all the salespeople in the Fortune 500 companies currently use such systems.

Now think about that desert island again. Even if you are wrong much of the time about the people you bring along, your friend will still be grateful that you made the effort. That's what every match in business, successful or not, will also result in: heartfelt thanks.

✳

While networking may seem like a random process of meeting people, recalling names, scooping up business cards, and eating an occasional meal, you'll do best if you follow a system such as mine, which is composed of (1) **collecting,** (2) **connecting,** and (3) **disappearing.**

The first part of this system is **collecting** the right people for your network.

In his book *The Circle of Innovation,* Tom Peters relates the story of McKinsey Group alum Allen Puckett, who gathers faculty members for his own "personal university." This is how he does it: He reads a stimulating article in a business journal or newspaper, calls the authors out of the blue, and invites them to dinner. Usually, they accept. The next time he finds himself facing a tough problem, he calls one of these "faculty members" from his university. And more often than not, he finds his solution. Just like the staff of a real university, Allen Puckett's personal faculty are the spokes on a great wheel of community learning.

Collection works best when it's done with the under-lying philosophy that every person is potentially relevant to you and your network. Don't screen anyone out. Sometimes people who may appear powerless or insignificant are potential stars waiting to rise. Someday they may become a key node in your network. And they will remember that you were on their side before they went large. People who judge their potential connections by their present status may be kissing their future good-bye. You never know where that one node may lead you.

In my case, a single person was what I call my node zero, or that one early connection without whom I wouldn't be writing this book today. This man is Kyle Smith, now an account executive at Yahoo!, and one of my early littermates at Broadcast.com in 1997. I met Kyle at a time when I'd just started woodshedding (holing up with as much to read as possible), learning all the theories I could and spraying them on anyone who would listen.

One of my bosses had asked me to be the keynote speaker at a morning sales meeting, so at 6:45 A.M., over doughnuts and coffee, with all of four months' experience under my belt, I evangelized Kevin Kelly's *New Rules for the New Economy* for my bizmates, explaining why we must all organize and leverage our relationships as a network in order to create long-lasting value.

My message struck a nerve with Kyle, who had just completed one of Broadcast.com's biggest deals yet with a printing company called World Color. He decided to turn me on to the World Color guys to see if there was a loose grain of wisdom in my books for them.

I sat down with a few of World Color's sales and executive types and, preaching the information economy rules, dropped several Big Thoughts. Soon I had their heads spinning with optimism about the digital future. They went back to World Color and told a division president, Tom Oliva, that he had to meet me.

Tom and I hit it off like Thelma and Louise, and we immediately launched into a conversation on what was important to both of us—new technology. World Color, one of the world's largest providers of print services, was trying to cope with the Internet and its non-paper premise. The company had two options: stick its head in the sand, or study digital technology and the Internet until they owned it so thoroughly they could teach their clients how to make the transition from paper to digital, ensuring that they would remain loyal to World Color even in a new and potentially threatening environment.

This is one company that was hungry for knowledge—and they were willing to act on that hunger.

In the meantime World Color opened its network to me by introducing me to Tom Peters and the speaking-seminar outfit Wyncom in March of 1999. Tom also liked what I had to say and he, too, offered me his network. He also gave me a speaking gig, letting me open for him at the kickoff of his Work Matters! movement. I was on my way.

On seeing all this, Kyle decided to spin a second thread and handed me to his friend Michelle Lemons, president of the International Speakers Bureau. I then had the consummate lovefest with her, trotting out my usual suspects of books and evangelizing them all. Two days later she insisted I meet Jan Miller, a literary agent who had been profiled in *The New Yorker*. We had a jiggy time together and Jan not only decided to represent me, she too opened up her Rolodex, which included fitness guru Jake Steinfeld, newscaster Maria Shriver, and best-selling author Dr. Phil McGraw. Thanks to Kyle, I now had an agent, a book deal, and a new network of opportunities.

Every node zero is out there. But if you miss the opportunity to connect with him or her because you're not paying attention, or the person doesn't seem deluxe enough, you may not get a second chance. Never let opportunities fly past. Always be in collection mode. Just as you always listen for insert points to share knowledge, always look for new contacts.

Here are five tips on how to be a great collector.

TIP 1: PREPARE THYSELF.

First, decide how best to organize your contacts. Do you scribble notes in an address book? That's hardly high tech, but it will do for the time being. Do you use a Palm Pilot? Maybe you have a simple contacts manager software program, such as ACT or Microsoft Outlook. The point is, get a system, any system, that makes you comfortable and gives you the ability to look up names easily.

If you don't have a system yet, start with a digital one. It's not expensive. You can invest as little as $75 by going online to any auction site and purchasing an old Palm Pilot.

Personally, I like compatibility. I use ACT (by Symantec) and I put every name into it religiously. (ACT even knows to save itself if you accidentally close it. And there are numerous sites online where you can use a free address book or briefcase to back up data, available to you no matter where you are.)

For those of you who are software-impaired, enroll in a course, like the one I had to take: a one-day, $40 class on how to use ACT.

Once you have a place where you can store your contacts, enter the basics: each person's name, company, title, department, fax and cell phone numbers, address, and so on. Place these in the top half of your form. The bottom half will consist of notes, groups, previous contacts, e-mail threads.

I prefer to categorize people into six basic groups: coworkers, peers, customers, family, music fans, and specific trade-conference attendees—but I have the capacity to expand these into more than one hundred different categories if the need arises.

Another 80/20 rule: 80 percent of all bizpeople working 40 hours a week and making over $30,000 a year use some sort of contacts management system. If you haven't joined them yet, now's the time to leave behind the 20 percent who don't.

Note: Many of us forget to carry our value around with us—in other words, we don't have our address book handy when connections are being made. That's why people say, "I'll have to get back to you later." It's a mistake. For years I used to print out my address book from my computer and carry it with me. Before that, I took my little black book with every address I needed in it. Today I carry an electronic organizer. Between my Palm Pilot and my cell phone, I can connect anyone I meet with anyone else in my network almost instantaneously.

TIP 2: SWAP.

No matter what you do or who you are, carry business cards. Swap these cards just as you'd swap recipes or stock tips. Anytime you make a major connection, swap. Anytime you make a minor connection, swap. If the other person doesn't have a card, hand out one of yours and have him or her write the requisite information on the back. You will lose many terrific potential contacts if you don't include this simple step in your system. Just place your contact's card in a designated new-card stack, an area inside your wallet, purse, or briefcase where you transport cards safely back to your work area, where you can enter them into your system. Or, give the other person your card and ask him or her to send you an e-mail. Most people's contact information is contained in their e-mail signature, so you can fill in your forms from there.

Always be in swap mode. Always believe you are just about to trade a Marv Throneberry for a Mickey Mantle.

TIP 3: ORGANIZE.

If you're not conscious of your business cards' value, you may wind up stashing them randomly in pockets or purses, losing most of them in the long run. Store business cards in a dedicated place on your person wherever you are.

Likewise, if you don't have a space in your work area dedicated to new cards, you may end up with an old shoe box full of them. And the bigger it grows, the more freaked out you'll get dealing with it. I've seen people leaving jobs staggering under the weight of boxes brimming with undigested business cards. There's something inherently unbusinesslike about that image. When you accept a contact's card, you aren't promising to hide it in some box. You are pledging some kind of future contact.

TIP 4: INPUT.

Input every Monday afternoon, or the moment you return from a business trip, or on the first day of the month—you must employ these kinds of rules to build your contact system. When the card stacks are small, you can input the information into your organizer without pain. And because they're still new, you'll recall relevant information about the person and identify the weak tie that got your conversation going. (The greatest people with the most powerful networks learn how to develop *weak ties*. Maybe you're a World War II buff and you meet someone else with the same affinity—that's a weak tie, but it's strong enough to create a vibrant conversation that can bind two people even if they have little else in common. Include these recollections in your notes.)

Be specific. Too many times we just jot down, "She works for So-and-So." That's not enough. I'll write, "Jane Doe was sitting next to me on a flight to Chicago while I was reading about brand leadership and she asked me why I was making so many notes. We started a conversation on personal atrophy and it turns out she's a human resources manager. She also loves U2 and she plays bridge." In my record, that note will help me in any subsequent conversations.

TIP 5: FOLLOW UP.

A simple idea. If you think it's appropriate—and it usually is—send your new contacts a note via e-mail. Tell them it was great to meet, and mention something about your connection: the weak tie, a common friend, whatever. Maybe this is the time to prescribe a book based on his or her function or place in the value space. You might even consider sending a book—an expensive offering, but one with high impact.

✳

Once you have collected people, the next step is **connecting** them. In other words, take your assortment of contacts and think about ways in which they can be linked.

You have to put work into this—you can't sit back and expect it to happen by itself. The process of connection is highly proactive. So are most successful people. Yahoo! vice chairman Tim Koogle talks about the difference between being active and being passive—or what he calls the story of "ing" versus "ed." If you spend time with people who say, "We are talking about that," "We are thinking about that," "We are planning that," be wary. These people aren't good bizpartners. They don't execute. People who say, "We studied it," "We planned it," "We did it" are the winners you should give your time to.

You only need a small number of contacts to start connecting. But despite the fact that business matches are easier to make than personal ones, be discerning. You can't randomly match everyone you meet. People who put together poor matches waste time. They damage their credibility and their personal brand.

Whenever you're ready to connect your contacts, think of them as belonging in one of three buckets. Some are partners. Some are peers. Some are prospects. Partners are people with whom you can have a deep business relationship; peers are people you do business with; prospects are those you hope will someday make partner or peer. Partners are the strongest tie. Prospects are the weakest.

It took some time to develop this habit, but now, whenever I've connected with a new contact, whether in a cafeteria, on a plane, or in the gym, I immediately think about whom I can connect this contact with, and from which bucket the connection will come. I might think, "I know someone at another company working on an architectural project just like this—maybe the two of them can get together and partner to reduce costs." Or, "I have a friend who is developing a new business that might be of interest. They might be great prospects."

There are two important points to keep in mind when connecting people. The first: Tune your receivers. The second: Fuse the connection.

First, **tune your receiver**: Train your ears to pick up subtle cues in conversation. Focus your attention. Listen for people's value—i.e., what they do or what they offer. And listen for their needs: i.e., what they want.

In every conversation I tune my receiver to filter out all the blah-blah of background noise and instead listen to the speaker's energy level, tone, and inflection to pick up excitement, anxiety, or any other emotion. Let's say I have several great contacts who are financial advisers. If, every time you talk to me, you mention the stock market, and as you do the tone of your voice rises to a fever pitch, you're not actually saying so, but I can tell you're freaked out by market volatility. That might trigger me to introduce you to my friend who's a steadfast financial adviser.

I also try to listen for words such as "need," "wish," or "aspire." These are all clues that people have some deep-seated desire that can help you make a real connection.

The act of listening is absolutely critical to the act of connecting, because if I truly understand what you do and what you require, as we have future conversations I will be able to connect you with someone who needs your value, or someone who has value for your need.

Note: Match people against their social velocity. Some people are extroverted, some introverted. The introverts do better with other introverts in your network. And less will mean more to them in terms of how many people you introduce them to. These people may feel overwhelmed if they have too many contacts; they have learned over the years how to wring the most out of the few they have.

Look at your node's character. Does Person A recoil at sexism? Well, Person B is a chauvinist. Don't put them together. Examine each person's bizneeds. Here's a guy whose little shipping company is failing: Should you find him a banker who'll pump money into his dying company? No.

Think before you link.

✳

And pinpoint a good reason to link. You don't want to be considered intrusive. When a telemarketer calls you at home at 10 P.M., or when some Internet scammer sends you an e-mail about his triple-X-rated site, it seems like an invasion of your privacy. We describe it that way because these marketers are giving us poor return on our attention, interrupting us with information we don't need. But let's say you're walking down the street and are about to enter a restaurant when someone makes an announcement aimed specifically at you, pointing out a better and cheaper restaurant just fifty feet away. This information is valuable, not intrusive.

In every appropriate conversation I think about my collection of contacts. I play it like a game. You mention problem, I think solutions—and I think about solutions in terms of people. For example, if I hear you worrying about refinancing your home mortgage, I conjure up my friend Batzi, who has amazing home finance contacts. And he's a lovecat. That's a match. I transfer the match to conversation—I say, "You need to meet Batzi. Here's his phone number. Let's call him right now."

Don't dawdle. Life happens fast. If you reflect on yesterday's conversations, you'll recall hearing about several of your bizmate's opportunities, problems, and needs. Think about the people you know who can provide them with solutions. Now learn to make these connections in real time. If you do, you can immediately suggest the network introduction in the context of their need. Most of the time your bizmate will readily agree to meet or talk with your contact.

Matchmaking is best accomplished on the spot. If I realize that someone in my network matches your needs, the more rapidly I express it, the better. Isn't it amazing we bumped into each other! I know just the right person for you! The faster I make the match, the less time others have to think of me as calculating. If you take four days to come up with a name, you can cause consternation: What was he really thinking? What is he really up to?

So immediately think: How can my network help? Can some node fill this person's needs? She says she needs someone to organize her books. You mentally scan your system and produce results. John Doe! He just left the XYZ Accounting Corporation. He's a great guy; he's perfect for her.

The most important part of speed: You don't miss connections. People with a need that you can resolve with a well-placed friend are like great house listings; they won't be around for long. Several times in the past I procrastinated before connecting two nodes, and by the time I did, one no longer had the need and the other no longer had the solution.

Speed is also important because, thanks to technology, aptitude can become obsolete quickly. So when you meet people who have talents that add value, get them hooked up today. Tomorrow their skills may not be as useful.

As you create new connections, you create even more benefits and needs. When I introduce two people who conduct business together, they'll often need several more partners along the way, which means that they require still more introductions to help them finish what they started. Let's say I introduce an entrepreneur to a chef. The entrepreneur has always wanted to invest in a restaurant and the chef has always wanted her own bistro. The moment they agree to cooperate, they'll need a real estate agent, a banker, an insurance agent, designers—all of whom I happen to have in my network.

Now, on to the other point: **Fuse the connection.**

Most of us think that once we connect, we're done. But many connections are merely passive, prospective associations. "You should look him up someday." "Sometime I'll introduce you guys." "You really ought to give her a call." These vague intentions have an astronomically high failure rate because people don't follow up on them. Such comments aren't even a significant addition to the conversation. They are filler.

Being active means becoming firmly involved. If I see a potential connection, I may call one of my nodes and vigorously sell him on the opportunity. If I am going to recommend a lawyer to you, I'll call her and say, "I just gave your name to Johnny Jones; he's a great guy and he's looking for someone to straighten out his legal complications, and I know that you're looking for a good opportunity."

My node gets that call from me *before* she gets the call from my contact, because I do everything I can to lend my brand to that connection. One of the most powerful statements I can make is "This guy is a good person whom you can trust." That represents significant commitment—a promise—on my part. It is, in effect, cobranding. I lend my brand to that person and I, and my reputation, live or die by it.

There are three excellent means of making these introductions. The most effective is person to person (or P2P). I arrange a meeting for the three of us, and the encounter is involving and direct.

The second way is by phone. Here you put together a conference call. I did this recently with my friend Tom Oliva, whom I was helping to network in Silicon Valley. He had left his job as president of World Color Retail to become president of a new start-up called E-Cargo; his new technology was a small penlike device with a tiny scanner at its end that, when scanned over any bar code from any product, could be hooked to a computer through a little cradle. It then requested information about the product, or ordered it online.

During one of my meetings with Tom it occurred to me that my friend at Jobs.com was looking for a big break-through. What about this idea: Someone reading the classified ads could scan a job posting with Tom's pen, and if the posting had a bar code, the résumé could be auto-matically sent in.

I pulled out my cell phone and Palm Pilot, looked up the Jobs.com business-development manager, and dialed. After telling him about Tom's technology, I handed Tom the phone and the two began a conversation. I then walked away. By the time I came back ten minutes later, they were setting up their first meeting. The result: They developed an independent relationship.

(Tom has since moved on again, this time to become president of the billion-dollar-a-year Moore Forms and Labels Corporation, a job he got through the CFO of Moore, a long-standing node in his own network.)

The third way of facilitating introductions is e-mail. This method I learned from Julie Anixter, currently man-aging director of research and development and new media at tompeterscompany! I first met Julie when Broadcast.com was producing a webcast for Wyncom, where Julie was work-ing. Julie connects people by means of three-way e-mail.

This is how she introduced me to the person responsible for convergence at Borders Books, Mary Jean Raab: She sent each of us an e-mail basically saying, "Tim, meet Mary Jean. Mary Jean, meet Tim," and then explained why we should know each other. It was an opportune introduction and we were both grateful.

Julie has introduced hundreds of people with her three-way e-mail approach, and her feedback tells her it's been highly successful. I now emulate her. This was a relatively easy way to make sure that the nodes in your network who should meet, do meet.

Note: A good lovecat is always thinking of ways to bring people together. For instance: Share your opportunities with your network. One friend of mine gets at least a half-dozen calls from headhunters every month. Each time he tells them to send him an e-mail, and when they do, he searches his network for someone who might like that job, refers them to the headhunter, and then introduces them via e-mail. That's a great way to take an intrusion and turn it into a connecting opportunity.

*

The final step, after collecting and connecting, is **disappearing.**

The idea: You remain active only until these relationships can survive on their own. Think of it this way: An obstetrician delivers the baby and stays around long enough to make sure that it is healthy. She doesn't raise the child.

So, get out of the connection as soon as you're sure it has fused. And tell your nodes you're doing so. They probably won't believe you. It doesn't matter. Say clearly and up front: "I think you need each other. I only want you both to be successful. I want nothing else from this. This is about you."

For example, if a connection takes place on a conference call I make with one of my nodes present, the magic follows when I let the other parties talk; I then leave the room. If I've arranged a three-way meeting, here, too, I will be the first to leave. Always drop off as early as is polite once you have properly fused the connection.

You must reduce the friction in all transactions. This is the key to understanding the future of business.

The Internet has boomed in part because of the friction that occurs in brick-and-mortar commerce transactions. Let's say you go to the store. There you find what you want, but when you make your purchase, you're not just paying for your product. You're paying various middlemen who have been involved along the way: the people who stored the product at the warehouse, or oversaw its transportation there, or sent it to the retailers—all of whom take out a percentage of the cost. The fundamental difference between buying something in a store and buying something online is the presence of these middlemen; they all create friction, which raises the price of the product. It's a necessary evil.

The same applies to business relationships. When you introduce two people, and you anticipate that they will create value, you normally expect something tantamount to a finder's fee. Think of that finder's fee as a price added into every deal you broker. People accept your introductions, but they maintain their guard based on the friction; you're a necessary evil to their doing business.

For most of us, the idea that relationships are brokered is baked into our bones, part of our genetic business code. We've learned it by watching consultants, for example, or the agency model, where a number of points always come off the top to pay these folks.

So as a bizperson, when you introduce two people and produce value, you have been taught to feel that you should capture some of that value, and usually even ask for it up front. This is one of our earliest lessons in the old economy: If you don't throw down the gauntlet, people will screw you.

The problem with this model is that it adds extra cost to the transaction. Each party has to consider that price and its hassle factor when they accept your offer to make introductions. Some people will even learn that because you are always asking for your share, it's better to ignore your introductions than to face the price.

Brokering also clouds the accuracy in matchmaking. If I'm too eager to extract my share from introductions, I set up too many of them. It's the old spaghetti-on-the-ceiling ploy—if you throw enough spaghetti into the air, some of it will stick. This phenomenon, in turn, reduces the attention people in my network will pay me when I say, "You've got to meet this person." After a while, they realize they don't have to.

Brokering relationships decreases the number of times people will accept your introductions, because when people see you coming, they have to take the cost of working with you into consideration. Not only will they stop following up on your suggestions, they'll filter you out, and your network of connections actually shrinks.

But just as the Internet vastly reduces friction because it allows the manufacturer a direct connection with the consumer at a low cost, so lovecats devastate friction in introductions. This is accomplished by disappearing after the connection is fused. People accept your introductions more readily than others' because they know you don't want anything from them. And in business, that's a very attractive value proposition.

Another advantage is scale. If you disappear after a connection, you can create a platform where your network multiplies itself—because when the matchmaking requires less time, you can match that many more nodes. You don't have to monitor whether or not they get traction, or interfere in the day-to-day misunderstandings that occur in most relationships. You don't have to lend your personal bandwidth to those bumps in the road. After all, if all an architect does is plan the house and supervise its building, he can create many more homes than if he had to hammer every nail and place every board.

Still another advantage to your disappearing act: efficiency. The most practical relationships are those that are forged when the motives are the purest. It's much more time-consuming to broker a deal than it is to create a relationship. It takes just a second to introduce my friend Tommy to my friend Terry. It could take me days to figure out how I could get something out of their interaction, negotiate an optimal deal, and then capture the prize.

When you lower the cost of accepting your introduction, you receive higher attention. You become a trusted source of information. And when you are trusted, people listen to you with preference, well ahead of other messages cluttering their lives.

✳

A well-executed connection is almost always a pleasure for everyone involved. Lovecats revel in the element of delight and surprise they can bring to the table. They thrive in their ever-expanding network.

Here's a caveat: You do run the risk that some people may rub their hands together with glee like Ebenezer Scrooge after they've profited from their connection, leaving you out in the cold. But think about it this way: You've got a job. You're not in the business of introducing, say, real estate guys to corporate guys. Your cost is zero. If you get nothing out of it, your loss is also zero. So even if you get scrooged four out of five times, that one time people reward you for your generosity is nothing but upside for you.

There are other forms of failure. Sometimes we make the hookup without a hitch, but then our contacts shrug their shoulders and go their separate ways.

Let it go. You don't really lose. That's part of the no-cost formula. You aren't keeping a balance sheet.

When you do hear about a failure, it's an opportunity to get feedback about where you went wrong. Maybe you need to understand personal chemistry better, or you need to listen more closely to other people's needs. When great salespeople fail to make a sale, they don't complain or give up. They ask, "What did I do wrong?"

Lovecats are in the business of getting others to trust us, to let us become a positive force in their lives. There will be times when you may feel this trust has been violated, but that's the great news about working with intangibles—you didn't lend out something you can't get back. You didn't give out your money, you didn't give away your car, you still have your wealth.

Although I don't count on it and I don't plan it, rewards happen. Some people I have placed together have gone out of their way to repay me by offering up their own intangibles: bringing me into new relationships, giving me new knowledge. Still, all in all, bizlove means never having to say "You owe me."

*

If a lovecat can hook you in to his or her network and there's no cost to you, that's not added value: That's multiplied value. It's like the difference between copy machines and fax machines. The more copy machines people bought, the more copy machines they had. The cost was the same to use them and their value did not grow. Period. But as people bought more fax machines, connections became possible among more and more people until everyone had to have a fax machine. That's multiplied value.

Eventually we are all going to build our own personal Internets and enjoy the same increasing returns provided by the existing Internet. The Internet became big just as other technologies based on increasing returns did. When the Net had only one hundred thousand users, it had a low overall value. As the numbers increased, it became more attractive to new users, causing it to grow larger. The Net soon took on a life of its own as millions logged on, in turn spending millions, increasing returns instead of diminishing them over time. The old diminishing-returns model, which applied to such marketing fads as the Pet Rock, works the other way—at some point demand ends and you're out of business.

Remember Metcalf's Law: The value of a network grows in proportion to the square of the number of users, which means that once a network achieves a certain size, it becomes almost irresistibly attractive.

One of the reasons why Microsoft was able to emerge as one of the world's biggest companies was this same increasing-returns model. Think of their software products as an intangible based on knowledge: the code and programming, which were invented by a group of highly intelligent developers. Initially, Microsoft sold its software at a low profit margin because it had to repay its up-front investment against knowledge (research and development). But once that debt was paid, the product, by becoming popular, became still more popular, and continued to sell long after Microsoft earned back all the money it had spent on developing the original software code. And the user base keeps multiplying: As new people purchase the software, an increasing number of others will have to do the same, because they need to be compatible with one another in order to exchange documents, presentations, and reports. At the same time, it costs Microsoft less money to make each copy of its programs.

The bigger it gets, the bigger it gets. The same is true for your network. Through the powerful word-of-mouse, love springs eternal in the connected world. Word-of-mouth equals incremental growth. Word-of-mouse equals exponential growth. This is a form of traction that is playing out over and over again in the Internet-based sector. Someday this will be true for all of us: Our network will equal our net worth.

IV

COMPASSION

Frankly, I fell into the final intangible by accident. It began with a simple realization: I had started letting people know how much I cared about them—my own particular exclamation point to my lovecat ways. I wasn't just acting as maven or matchmaker. I was becoming emotionally involved. I was being human—on the job! And this display of genuine emotion, I realized, was having a beneficial effect on my bizlife.

I'd always tried to be a caring person, but I'd never been particularly warm at work. The reason? I couldn't stand the thought of all the ridicule, cynicism, or rejection I might face. In the business world this is known as a barrier-to-entry.

But that barrier fell when I was an account executive at Broadcast.com. As mentioned, once I began to show my love for Ken Weil and Tim Plzak at Victoria's Secret, I realized that this was not some secondary, after-hours part of our relationship, but a primary driver of success in our day-to-day business. My willingness to commit myself to these people openly and firmly helped them understand that I wasn't selling them a bill of goods. I was sharing my heart because I truly cared as much for their success as I cared for my own. A good lovecat, I was realizing, is only as good as his lovemates.

It didn't happen quickly. While Tim was a hugger before I ever knew him, Ken warmed up to hugging slowly. But when he embraced me after the first Victoria's Secret webcast, I knew that both of us had become out-of-the-closet, out-in-the-open, out-of-this-world lovecats. This was new for Ken, too. Now he was asking me about my wife, my music, my life; we were developing a genuine bond. Tim and Ken both held a special place in their hearts for me, and vice versa. Business was becoming a new experience, one in which my heart was involved as much as my head.

I soon began to behave similarly toward my other biz-contacts and bizmates. I became more emotionally open. I hugged people. I was a two-fisted handshaker. I made eye contact. I smiled. I opened my mouth and instead of just recommending a book or a bizcontact, I also expressed my feelings for the people I met in my day's journey. Anyone could turn out to be a Ken Weil in my life.

Here are some of the statements I dared to say:

"I am totally committed to your personal growth."

"Thanks for being such an incredible person."

"I only want you to be happy, and that's what is going to drive this deal."

"I love you, man. You are a rock star."

So what if some people laughed? So what if some people thought I was just sucking up? Or sucking down? Or sucking sideways? The knowledge and the network—these are value-added and easy. Share the books, share the Palm Pilot; you can be fairly certain that these will be well-received and credible gifts. But consider sharing compassion! Consider overcoming the cold and impersonal behavior between clock-in and clock-out hours, consider conquering the urge to be noncommittal when it comes to feelings!

Most of us don't feel comfortable with workplace intimacy. But I say you've got to express your compassion, because, combined with knowledge and network, it is the way we win hearts and influence business in this, the dawn of the new business world.

Furthermore, unlike knowledge and network, compassion is a resource that each of us already possesses. Maybe you haven't read a book in fifteen years and you're daunted by the task because you fear it will take years to gain enough knowledge to be knowledge-added (but of course it won't). You may also think you won't be able to make enough new connections to create your own personal explosion of network circuits (that, too, is not true).

Yet no matter where you are in your career, you know that you can listen to people, you can support them, you can hug them. Compassion is something you can practice even before you finish this book.

Being compassionate presents lovecats with a unique opportunity. People tend to fear intimacy in business because they fear embarrassing themselves. No one wants to be known as some high-fiving, happy-hugging, crazy dude, because no one takes that person seriously. An unstable image is not an issue for lovecats, however. Because we lead with our knowledge and our network, we can close with compassion because we have already established our credentials. Compassion is the icing on an already excellent cake.

Lovecats don't just give you what you need—we *are* what you need.

✳

Why should you show compassion in the workplace?

For starters, **there is a tremendous opportunity for your compassion to make a difference in how people view you, and how they view themselves.**

Most of us are kenneled at work—we sit in cube farms filled with prairie dogs: If a commotion occurs somewhere within the farm, all the dogs poke their heads out of the cubes to look.

These cold rows of cubicles are hard to personalize. There is almost no room to post photos, pin up belongings, or make the cubes feel like home. Every component of our workspace is wired, efficient, and operates at the speed of light. But compared to our dad's corner office, which was inefficient in terms of space but excellent for discussions, closed-door meetings, and private get-togethers, everything is cold.

Work life is transitory, too. Ideas are formed, created, and die in the space of one person's working life. People come and go like the weather. As a result, long-term loyalty to companies is eroding. (But at the same time, our short-term loyalty can be ferocious, because we are all in a heated battle against the competition to accrue as much money, stock options, and other perks as quickly as possible.) The odds are that you may never emotionally move in to your job.

Sometimes it seems that no one's even talking. We now use myriad electronic tools to communicate—e-mail, instant messages, voice mail, faxes—instead of holding person-to-person conversations. We may never hear the sound of our peers' voices and never see their signatures, our most individual mark.

We are squeezing out of business that inefficient, no-ROI thing called humanity. We no longer stop to ask people how they are, we seldom celebrate personal success, we fear touching people in a world of sexual-harassment litigation. We are wringing all that is human out of the workplace like we squeeze water from a sponge, and we do it in the name of business. Then it seems that bosses and consultants go out and read more books on how to depersonalize the workplace even further.

If you discovered that your children were being schooled in architecturally cold buildings and placed in isolated cubicles, you'd protest. Nor would you intentionally raise your kids in a transitory environment where they change schools every year, see fewer and fewer other kids, and never get a gold star or an A. You'd predict that such children would end up dysfunctional. But do humans ever really stop growing? We may stop developing physically somewhere between the ages of eighteen and twenty-five, but we develop emotionally and spiritually until the moment we die.

Just because we're at work doesn't mean that we're not human; sometimes we need someone to touch us, to make us smile, to make us feel better about ourselves. According to the late Mother Teresa, the greatest disease in the West is not tuberculosis or leprosy; it is being unwanted, unloved, uncared for.

Since people are basically utilitarian, they value others for their ability to fill these basic needs. When you do, you're providing a service no one else in business offers. You become the person who makes other people feel good. It's as if you were selling a product worth a dollar, for a penny. In fact, your compassion makes others view you in a way that money can't buy. You are so money you don't even know it!

Because many in powerful positions don't understand this concept, they minimize it. They place value on other skills that they grasp more fully, such as seniority, or exclusivity, or power. But for the most part they don't tend to be people whom others want to work for, and they don't tend to inspire great loyalty.

But others understand compassion masterfully. Look at the CEO of SouthWest Airlines, Herb Kelleher. He is an original lovecat. This man will hug you on the day you need it the most, beam a smile at you when you are down in the dumps, tell you that you're a Michelangelo at whatever position you hold at his company. His managers value that same level of compassion in their employees. During job reviews, the company finds that those who make others feel good about themselves—and who are good at their jobs—are most worthy of promotion. It's for good reason that SouthWest's stock trades on the New York Stock Exchange under the symbol LUV.

Compassion will lead to a better experience with your bizmates.

Let's say we're working in the same office, and you're having one of those quintessential bad days. It's gray outside, you haven't slept well, you have a headache, your boss just threw a tantrum, and on and on and on. I walk into your cube and show you compassion. I hug you (if you like being touched), I compliment you (if you like being praised), I smile at you (if you like being beamed at). Everything about what I do—the way I listen, my tone of voice, my facial expressions—makes you feel better. You walk off to grab a cup of coffee, and as you come back to your cube you pass mine, and now, because you're feeling good, you beam those feelings back to me. Lo and behold, maybe I was feeling depressed, too, but was hiding it. Now I'm recharged. The next person who comes into my cube—maybe a customer, maybe another coworker—is also down, but now that I'm jacked up from your positive feedback, I can share my improved mood. I can even have an incredible day. I'm electric!

The other day someone asked me, "Where do you get all your energy?" Without a pause I replied, "From the feedback I get from other people." It is my fuel. I live to create value in people's lives and I measure myself by their reactions. I'm a love merchant. I trade in intangibles. I can trade that currency to infinity. Maybe I'm relating current events to a new book I've just read on branding, and someone reacts by sharing personal anecdotes as well as an article she's just read in *AdWeek*. It's a two-way blast as I give her a book to read and she tells me the essence of her experience. To me, this is a wonderful validation. The tones of our voices spin upward and something magical happens in that short time we spend together. We are both electric!

Consider a good coffee shop's bottomless cup. You stagger inside the café, slide into a booth, and the waitress puts down an empty cup; after your grunt or nod, black coffee pours into it. You mix the coffee to taste as you read, talk, or eat, and the cup stays full. No extra cost. All you can drink. You are fully awake now, and you are charged. A lovecat is that cup and the service experience of having it poured freely.

A bottomless cup of wake-up is a constant source of energy, inspiration, and optimism. If an acquaintance smiles at you, it's because you were good for his head and his heart last time he saw you. It's a stimulated response. It means that both of you can go off and do your job with more energy, more vitality, and more zest than if neither of you had exchanged that pleasant moment. Who doesn't do better work when they're charged up?

Remember, if your style is to share entertainment value, it is rare that you get back a matching joke at the same level every time. If you feed someone's greed, it is rare to nonexistent that your own greed is fed in return. But a smile equals a smile. It is highly likely that as we stop and share compassion with others, giving them all our ebullient energy, people will like us back. Sharing compassion is a contagious activity. You will experience more hugs that are exclusive to you. You will see more smiles than other people. You will be touched more. You will have more excellent experiences in a world where excellence is rare.

By expressing your compassion, you create an experience that people remember. When people remember you, it's good for your business.

An experience is a private event that occurs in response to external stimulation: When you eat a bowl of particularly delicious ice cream, when you meet your favorite celebrity, when you hear one of those extraordinary high notes that opera singers reach, a personal moment is triggered in your head and your heart.

As mentioned earlier, the ability to create an experience can jet-propel your career. It raises your value and drives your price. The truth is, we are all marketing ourselves every day. Being likable is a large part of this personal marketing—work is easier if people are drawn to you. And as we've moved from a service economy to an experience economy, we have shifted our focus from the benefits a product or service provides to the type of sensations, or the experience, it creates.

Now transfer that theory back to yourself: Consider your bizlife as an arena in which to meet people and create a compelling experience for them. Caring is a great way to do that. As marketing folks say, packaging is everything. Think of the difference between calamari and squid—same thing, different prestige—and therefore a different price.

We seldom create memorable experiences through basic transactions. "Get a good deal." "Sign right here." "It'll be there next Tuesday." "Thank you very much, sir." That's straightforward business—no feelings, no sensations, except the occasional satisfaction of having saved money, as in, "Boy, did I get a great deal!"

In fact, when traditional business creates an experience, it's usually resource-dependent. For example, you can provide a limited experience based on your entertainment value—and we all know people who do this. They tell jokes, make funny quips, or dish great gossip. But the role of a clown is tough to maintain—only a few people are so funny or informed that they can sustain the interest of other people over time.

Other people feed the greed. They give discounts, break the rules, slip you free handouts to curry favor. But that role is also hard to maintain—eventually their false generosity eats into someone else's profits. Feeding the greed isn't a good way to differentiate, anyway; a lot of people are already struggling to occupy that space.

But if I communicate to you that I care about you, you are more likely to listen to what I say. People love to hear about themselves. Their attention spans sharpen when the discussion centers on them. The more you genuinely care about others, the more likely they are to open up their own channel capacity as a human being. In the bizworld, that's everything.

Whether what you have to offer is a person, a product, or a service, create the most compelling experience. People for whom you've created an experience will become your most avid salespeople. They will spread the good word about you. They will refer you business. Such referrals aren't just about the quality of your service or your product. People refer people who represent a good experience to them. Soon, instead of having a social circle, you'll have a spiral of raving, clicking fans.

Compassion creates commitment—which keeps you focused on building your knowledge and network.

When you tell people that you are committed to their success, you are making a promise. When you hug people, you are making a specific statement about how you feel. When you guarantee that you intend to make a difference in their bizlives, you are setting an expectation.

Your expression of compassion puts your intentions on the table. When you're in a business relationship and you've made it clear that you care for others, you cannot— you cannot!—let them down.

If you're cold and calculating (your basic what-have-you-done-for-me-lately type), you don't have anything to live up to. You haven't committed anything to any-one, so you don't have to care about a soul. When you're warm and compassionate, however, you cannot betray that expressed respect. You have committed yourself to helping others. (Remember ham and eggs: chicken = involved, pig = committed.)

That's not to say it's easy. All of us can become truly tired. We work all the time. We travel all the time. We don't get enough sleep. We approach the edge of burnout. It's hard for us to keep feeding our value by reading great books and building our networks. It's difficult to follow through with all of our attempts to share our networks. But we must. We promised. When you throw something out on the table like "I love you," you can't walk away.

Nor can you change your mind. Few things are more annoying in your personal or your professional life than a person who is warm one minute and cold the next. No matter the context, it hurts.

Be constant. Stay focused. It's as though every time you touch people in business, you are running for president of their heart, and you've got to keep your campaign promises.

Compassion buys forgiveness.

If you enjoy warm, compassionate relationships with your bizmates, you will be given a larger margin of error during those times when you are less than perfect—and all of us come up short at some point. Not that you should take undue advantage of this latitude. But it's like money in a rainy-day bank account: It's good to know it's there.

The less human we are, the more our partners value us based on sheer numbers. We don't give them any other yardstick. But when we make a genuine comrade out of a bizmate, forgiveness becomes natural, so that even when our circumstances change, we still care for one another, we still trust each other.

Think of the difference between the corner self-service gas station and your dry cleaner. You don't know a soul at the gas station and you'll stop at a different one when it's more convenient or offers a better price. But if you have a good, consistent relationship with your dry cleaner, they can raise their prices or you can move six blocks; you'll remain a patron because of your history. So even when my cleaners once lost a shirt—something that might normally send me into a fit—I forgave them because I liked them and because I trusted that they would eventually atone (which they did a few months later when I needed a suit cleaned and pressed in less than an hour; they did it happily).

Likewise, your business relationships have greater longevity when based on human feelings rather than circumstances. Again, Cisco Systems is a good example. Customers remain at Cisco even when Cisco makes mistakes (as everyone does in business now and then), because companies such as Cisco generously and relentlessly foster partnerships. People remember Cisco less as the company that sold them their equipment than as the company that, say, facilitated a partnership with B2B firm Ariba down the street by introducing them to that company's high-level players.

Likewise, Cisco frequently brings small companies into seminars in which they help elucidate the future, giving away free knowledge and creating an environment for these smaller firms to meet and build alliances. Most of the attendees are amazed that Cisco is willing to invest such money and time with no stated agenda for itself. Because of this, Cisco wears a halo, and its customers have little negative to say about it, even though Cisco probably has its fair share of mishaps.

*

Now that you understand the rationale for being compassionate, it's time to talk about how to become one of those purrrring lovecats who can change the world around them with their wily human ways.

Bear this in mind: Showing compassion is a process, not just an action. An action: writing someone a check, opening a door, introducing a friend to a friend. A process: making an effective, sustained long-term plan for showing compassion.

If compassion is just a single step, it happens almost by chance. You never really know why you took it; you don't remember your actions; you have no idea what kind of impact the gesture had.

But if you wish to be a true compassionary, practice compassion as part of a well-planned process whereby you always do your best and resolve to get even better. You work on your timing, the methods you use to express your compassion, your follow-up, and your closure. All of these are improved by experience when you see compassion as a two-part process—**sensing,** and **expressing**.

Sensing begins with a raw sensory experience. Someone approaches you and you perceive, through conversation or body language, possibilities that might allow you to bond, or a spark that causes you to feel an immediate affinity for this person. Whenever it happens to me, I picture an anteater reflexively snapping up a meal faster than the human eye can see. You must be prepared for these moments of intuition. They are few and far between. Keep your senses polished and primed throughout the day.

It's difficult for someone to teach you to have a great singing voice—that's an intrinsic talent—but a coach can show you how to sound better through vocal warm-ups, how to hit higher notes than you've ever hit before. The same idea applies here. I can't change your raw ability to sense other people's needs, but I can help you tune up the talents you already possess, just as a lawyer can better her skills at recognizing unacceptable clauses in a contract, or a quality inspector can become increasingly efficient at spotting product flaws. As a lovecat, you treat sensing as a professional skill, and constantly strive to improve your abilities.

True, some people are not very sensitive to others and may never be. But most of us are—especially effective bizpeople. We build that skill over time, morphing into quasi-private detectives, because if we are to be successful in business, we must learn to observe the world around us very, very carefully.

Still, many of us don't know what to look for. I certainly didn't until I actively went about being a better lover in business. And, keep in mind that there is no one way for all. It's personal; each one of us will have different ways to express our love and sense others' receptivity. Here are some tips to get you started:

Notice body language. People reveal everything over time; we all have repeated opportunities to see our contacts with their clients, their bosses, their assistants.

Everyone has their own version of body love. Some people are standoffish, others are always hugging or touching. Be observant. Watch how people react when a colleague enters a room. Some simply nod their head and emit a terse hello. Others get up and bestow a warm hug. One is a minimum gesture, the other a maximum. Figure out the minimum and the maximum where you're comfortable. Maybe you see a man hug his best customer when they meet before a conference, but when he greets you, he wipes his palms on the side of his pants before shaking your hand. Clearly he handles acquaintances differently from long-term friends.

Once you've observed others, you become aware of a dynamic range, allowing you to extrapolate where you stand between the one person they barely know and the one who is warmly embraced.

Some people are immediately approachable, and some are not. Don't mix the two up. Think of it like this: If someone appreciates soft music, and you want to play a song with a full crescendo, start with soft notes. You wait before you get to the crescendo. You blast your hard-rock-fan friends with that crescendo from the very first note, because anything else would lose their attention. The same goes for love.

Timing is everything. There's a right time and a wrong time to express your compassion verbally. Listen for cues. Eventually you will understand when you have permission to go off-topic with people.

Every person has his or her own conversational rules. Some people stay on message; the reason you are on the phone is the only reason you are on the phone. If they call you for price quotes on widgets, even if they call you every week, it's the same conversation each time, a structured dialogue with no wiggle room. These people make it difficult to express any compassion, ever. Live with it.

Others are more willing to stray off-topic. The most common insert points these people allow are the pregnant pauses that mark the beginnings of their conversation, because that's when people are most open to chat about something other than the business at hand. If nothing fills these pauses, once the business talk commences, the patter becomes too rapid. Don't let these opportunities fly past. Develop an instinct for those moments when people will let you slip personal topics into the conversation.

Anytime I sense that the expression of compassion is appropriate, I divert the talk stream. Maybe you've brought up the fact that it's pouring outside. I might ask, "Does that make you want to stay home and curl up by the fire, or do you feel like Kurt Cobain huddled under a bridge in Seattle?" You may admit to feeling as low as the late pop icon's description of his childhood. From there I might ask how the weather's been over the last seven days; when the answer comes back that it's been terrible, I might say, "The stock market's been equally gloomy." Soon I turn the conversation to how worried I am about your company. You now tell me that the attitude around your office is negative because of the plunging market. I say I'm truly concerned for you, and, reminding you how important you are to your company, and how much value your company brings to the industry, I do whatever I can to warm up your day.

Most business conversations are transactional. But when people stray off-subject, their force field temporarily comes down and doesn't go back up again until they return to the business at hand. It's during these moments that you have your best shot. True, some people never lower their guard. You try to get in, you fail. Conversational love can be shared only when it doesn't distract from the discussion of business.

But don't let clear feedback opportunities pass you by. Sometimes people will lob them like softballs you can knock over the fence—the most common being "How are you doing?" Probably no question is asked more and answered less in business.

One of my office buddies (and a recent lovecat convert) always answers my How-Are-You question with a sincere "I'm only doing okay if you're okay." He makes me feel special every time, even when I'm blue.

Now that you've honed your sensory instincts, it's time for **expressing**.

Lucky humans—we have so many ways to express our feelings, from looks to words to gestures. Countless books have been written on the subject, so consider this discussion simply cliffing the topic until, if you wish, you study it more fully.

Start with your eyes, an often-misused weapon in our nonverbal arsenal. My all-time number-one favorite lovecat writer, Leo Buscaglia, said that he always looked for what he called "kind eyeballs" in a crowd of strangers. They give you confidence, he says in his book *Love.* "Even if you are saying something stupid . . . they'll be saying, 'It's all right, man. Go on!'"

When you let others look directly into your eyes, it can feel as though they are looking right into your soul. That's why we think people can tell if we're lying when they see our eyes; it's also why we have such deep eye contact with our most intimate lovers. It may be the most direct form of communication humans have. The great Spanish writer Cervantes called eyes "the silent tongues of love."

Although bizpeople look at each other all the time, they seldom gaze into each other's eyes. It's a part of our culture. As columnist Ann Landers once said, "Television has proved that people will look at anything rather than each other." People look at foreheads, eyebrows, noses— anything but the eyes. So I make it happen. If I have to, I take my hands and grab someone's shoulders to stop both of our worlds long enough to make true eye contact. It's the strongest way to bond. It shows you are present and that you care.

Smile. Obvious? Most people forget to do it. Push yourself to smile when you greet or talk to others. Clearly it's not always appropriate; you don't smile when you know the other person won't like it or the situation doesn't call for it. But a smile has an amazing effect. Notice how rare and positive are those moments in your bizlife when people smile at you.

Think about what I call soul smiles. Everyone knows how to smile, although many flash a fake grin that is worse than no smile at all. People can tell when that flash of teeth is a lie. Some people, however, smile from their soul. It feels as comforting as when close friends hug you after a long absence. Smiles have that same effect when you take the time to think about them, when you let them radiate from deep within.

Express yourself with warm words. Too many people follow the impassive model set by the late Vince Lombardi, former coach of the Green Bay Packers. You could have been Lombardi's son and star on his football team, and you would have done well to get one little "atta boy" from him in a season. It wasn't in his self-interest to divulge his cards.

Such stoicism is baked into business, right up there with learning golf and wearing Dockers. Never let them know you want to buy it, never let them think you want to sell it, and never let them see you sweat. Some companies don't share information with their partners for the same reason—they think power is about keeping things private. I disagree.

Let's say a guy has worked for The Boss for eight years. He put in twelve-hour days when the crunch was on, he was always there whenever he was needed, he was a solid performer. But now he's under financial pressure. He hasn't had a raise in a year. He doesn't know his next step but senses he could do better elsewhere. He tells the boss he wants to leave. The boss likes the guy, but in his world he wouldn't say such a thing. So he clams up, says good-bye, and adds a cold "Good luck." He thinks that's enough emotion. But all his employee heard was that the boss didn't care. He walks out feeling even more unhappy than before. The boss feels sad, the guy feels sadder—they have a complete disconnect.

Our words color our bizlives. Make statements that are positive, committal, or possible. Many of us sound vague and ambiguous and put on a poker face even as we try to bathe others with compassion. How warmly can it register when you're trying to say "I deeply appreciate all the work you've done for me" but all you bark out is

"Good job"—and you're not even looking at the other person when you say it?

Here's a trick I learned from Leo Buscaglia: For a day, every time you're ready to use the word *hate,* try to substitute the word *love.* Watch the attitudes of your coworkers.

Let's say you work at an ad agency. An associate brings you a prototype of a project she's been slaving over. You say: "I hate work that's late. I hate neutral colors in advertising campaigns. I hate comps that aren't on pressboard." And maybe you're telling the truth in all cases.

But instead, try saying: "I love it when people let me know their work is going to be late. I love it when people go beyond using neutral colors. And I'd love it even more if this was on pressboard."

You're still making your point. You'll also be making your coworkers a great deal happier.

Express yourself now. Tell people you love them today. When I meet new contacts I often ask them to close their eyes and think about a person from their past or present professional life whom they care about—someone whom they have never told how much they care. Then I say, call that person right now—no matter where he or she is. For example, when I was selling this book to publishers, I was sitting in the office of my new friend, publishing honcho

Phyllis Grann, and I asked her: "Is there someone in publishing whom you love but have never told?" Just as she was thinking it over, a woman walked into the room, making Phyllis's eyes light up. "That's the person!" she said. "Right there! Susan!" Like a daytime talk-show host, I played love doctor on the spot. "Tell Susan you love her," I said. "She deserves it." What a scene, and what a feel-good day for Susan.

This drill is contagious. Connect people in a positive way, and it's like watering flowers—the love will sprout and blossom. In a recent meeting with my lovecats in the ValueLab, I asked each of them to think of five people at the company whom they cared for. Each one of my reports went to the whiteboard and wrote down names, giving a one-sentence summary of their friends' features and attributes. Then I pointed at the board and told the troops that these names represented the most important list they might ever see. I next asked each person in the Lab to circle one of the names they'd submitted. "That person has a special need for compassion," I said. "When this meeting disbands, contact that person and let them know you care."

Each of them went out and did as suggested, and each one came back and told me that the results were one very happy friend who hadn't been feeling quite as happy before.

Use your arms. I don't know who invented hugging—probably some lovecat primate eons ago—but not only is it a natural, wonderful gesture, it's vastly underemployed in the workplace. When we hug, we transfer energy, we sense each other's heartbeat, we make people feel closer to us. But a great deal of intelligent discretion is required here—the workplace can set up many obstacles to touch, and especially to hugging.

I've learned to hug in progression. I don't do it all unless I know I have permission. Then I start slowly. For my first hug, I put only a little strength into it, giving a kind of weak sideways squeeze. Eventually I use more force, and only when I am sure a person is comfortable do I hug as I would outside the workplace.

For example, I've been working on a new project with my friend Phyllis Grann, who is renowned for her professional demeanor. But I see her compassionate side. My first interaction with her was a simple, unthreatening sideways hug; since then I have slowly worked up to a strong two-armed embrace. Few people in publishing believe me, but Phyllis now hugs me warmly whenever we meet. If I don't initiate it, she opens her arms and invites me in, saying, "Tim, where's my hug?" It comes straight from her heart.

Of course, you must consider the situation. I would seldom hug someone who reports to me, or who works close to me in a physical space, or who has demonstrated itchiness against it. There are still plenty of people left to hug in this world. Just be smart about it.

Perfect your handshake. Handshakes also transfer excellent energy, especially when you mix them with a hug and/or a smile. But business has overemphasized the firm hand-shake. I believe in a comparable handshake. I want my shake to match others', in strength and in rhythm.

Observe how people shake hands, and record it in your mind as you get to know them over time. People have a reasonably consistent signature in their handshakes; they'll shake a hand similarly each time—the level of firmness, how high or low the hand reaches, how much movement they put in it. Develop a shake that replicates others', meaning that you match firmness, distance, and rhythm.

Don't forget the power of the second hand. The first time I shake hands with a new contact, I shake one hand. Eventually, as we become closer, I move over to two hands, and then try shaking the hand and touching the arm at the same time. There's just a little more commitment in the expression.

Always keep this in mind: You must be certain you have permission to touch someone before you do it.

When people enter a room, make it a point to look at them. When I first transferred over to Yahoo! and moved to California, I felt invisible. No one seemed to see me. I'd walk down halls or attend meetings and always feel alone. Then one day, when I walked into an important meeting, several people looked up at me and smiled. I knew I had arrived.

This is true for most people who start at a new job— you feel alienated until you break on through and people look right at you, making you feel at home.

Why take so long? Look at people who enter the room. You don't have to wait until they've been around for years. By doing so, you are making the first move toward compassion. You are saying: "I notice that you are present, I am glad you are here." That can make all the difference. At work my lovecats know I always recognize them when they come into a room; they like it. Now they do it for others, too.

Be prepared. Business offers us constant contact with other people, but how often do we have a chance to show some compassion during that contact? Most of these encounters are fast—fleeting e-mails, quick phone calls, chance meetings in hallways. But on those occasions when you have the opportunity to show compassion, do so. It doesn't happen very often. True long-term relationships often start with what look like small opportunities.

Be spontaneous. The longer you take to think compassion through, the less credible is its ultimate expression. If you act without hesitation, you are baring your soul. Even waiting a few minutes can seem wrong. After all, if your significant other tells you he or she loves you, you don't wait a day to reply, "I love you, too." You say so on the spot. Bizlove is no different.

> **Note:** Don't let desks, chairs, or tables get between you and bizlove. You don't need to sit on someone's lap whenever you want to talk, but as you begin a conversation with people whom you know you can touch, make a concentrated effort to walk around any physical obstacle and get close enough that you can make some form of physical contact.

As always, tune yourself to sense permission. Don't leap over a table to meet someone who doesn't want to touch you. Be smart when you play nice.

Once you have mastered your means of expression, you must search for **opportunities to express.** We've talked about the proper insert points to share your knowledge and your network. Now it's time to look for insert points to share compassion.

I can think of three primary insert points in business

relationships: **salutations, conversations,** and what I call **quick opps.**

Salutations

There's a new node in my network, Kevin Smith, who works at Kellogg in Michigan. We first became acquainted at a meeting where I was doing my standard lovefest. Afterward he told me how much he liked my energy. "Stay in contact with me and we'll do a lot together," he said. We shook hands, and with our good-byes we made a strong connection.

The next time I returned, I stood up and recognized Kevin with a beam as he walked into the room. He reached out to shake my hand, we talked about our families and our lives, and through that hello we reestablished our rapport. There was no reason not to show it to the world because we were both confident that our affinity was authentic.

Whenever I think of salutations, the old Doors song "Hello, I Love You" comes to mind. These salutations offer all kinds of opportunities for compassionate expression, because every time you say hello or good-bye in business you have permission to express yourself. Between hellos and good-byes, the average person has about twelve such opportunities a day—or six people, twice each.

That's 60 salutations a week; 240 a month; in a year, almost 3,000 opportunities.

What can you do with those opportunities? You can express yourself with your words, your energy, and your embrace.

First, make sure you recognize someone else as an individual. A large and growing body of research says that when you call people by name, you make them feel better about themselves. Dale Carnegie once remarked that most people find there's no sound more beautiful than the sound of their own name. And that means they pay more attention to it, and to you. (But don't overdo it—I've run into people who say my name so often, it sounds silly. As always, use discretion.)

Another approach: Predict a good conversation. When you greet people, tell them you are looking forward to talking with them, and foresee a good result.

Then ask a question, as part of your salutation: "How are you?" Make sure you offer a guaranteed listen. Too many people, when they ask about someone else's health, career, or family, move rapidly to their real question, one which usually concerns them. Nor do they exhibit any body language that says "I am listening." It usually says, "I couldn't care less about you."

Instead, when you ask a question, take a deep breath,

make eye contact, and lean forward in order to show that you're engaged. This sets the right tone for whatever will follow.

Or, confirm your feelings at the point of meeting: "I'm really glad to see you." "I'm always happy to spend time with you." "I look forward to the time we spend together."

Don't shy away from the bonding words that people often substitute for standard salutations. Most people have seen the Budweiser beer campaign with the phrase "Wassup?" The company took a short film in which four men greeted each other by using that phrase repeatedly and turned it into one of the most successful advertising campaigns in recent history—and made "Wassup?" the year's most popular bonding expression.

Some of these expressions are silly, but most words that charge other people usually are. Bonding isn't about the words themselves. It's about attitude. Use these words. Let them become currency. So even though a hundred million people have seen that Budweiser campaign, when some junior accountant throws off his glasses and yells "Wassup?", go with it, enjoy it, participate in it. Never lose the willingness to make light of yourself, or to have fun with others.

These expressions dot the culture and derive from television, sports, politics, entertainment—every part of our world. In the old TV series of the same name, the character Rerun used to ask, "What's happening?" This phrase conquered the bizworld, too. And when the New York Mets went to the World Series in 2000, their theme song was "Who Let the Dogs Out?" It seemed as though those words were on everyone's lips at each meeting I attended that fall. These bonding chants become old quickly, but when they're hot, they're fire.

Then there are the perennials, such as calling someone "my champion." Generally at least one person inside another company is your steadfast advocate. So when you walk into a meeting and see this person, you say, "My champion!" and shake with both hands. Those words don't seem to fade.

A shared bonding statement is the human equivalent of a dog rolling over on his back. It shows relaxation in demeanor, a letting down of the guard; you trust someone enough to make a slight fool of yourself.

Because we let salutations include touch and expression, you can build on them over time. Don't try to do everything at once. In *Permission Marketing,* Seth Godin says that if a man walked into a bar with a shiny diamond ring and proposed to every woman, all would reject him. But if he walked into the same bar and asked if he could buy someone a drink, he might obtain that first small permission to talk. Then, over much time, someone might give him permission to marry her. Having permission to get close to people is everything. You must start, however, with small permissions, such as shaking hands with both hands, making eye contact, smiling; all this provides you with a little piece of permission to build on.

Conversations

Conversations offer many varying opportunities for expression, whether you are riding in a plane, having lunch, or working with others on ongoing projects.

Most important to keep in mind: Frame your conversations with bizlove.

When you frame a picture, you surround it with a certain perspective. You can frame it with care or you can simply stick it on the wall. Sometimes you mat it, other times you place it in a gold-leaf frame that costs more than the picture itself.

To frame a conversation with compassion, surround it with perspective, too. Make it clear right away that the focus of the conversation is the benefit and happiness of the other person. Make a committed statement to that effect. This way, even the most chance conversations have the potential to become important to both of you.

Even if I'm having a ten-minute conversation, I frame it as strategic. Maybe you've come up with a new organizational idea, and I notice that it represents your ability to streamline your industry. We might then talk about how any one of us can fundamentally change our business, and your small idea begins to seem much bigger.

For instance, one of my fellow Yahoo!s, a manager with a small staff, approached me the other week. As in most companies, Yahoo! conducts reviews to discuss and evaluate employees' performance. This man, new at managing, wasn't confident in himself yet, so he asked his employees to write him a one-page note evaluating his management skills.

When he told me his idea—that you review yourself before you review others—I lit up. I then framed the conversation by putting together a series of facts and assertions that led to his small idea becoming a Big Thought. I told him it could have a tremendous impact on how his people felt about him and his abilities as a manager. Perhaps your coworkers will notice how this works, I said, and the virus will spread throughout the company, and more and more people will take up your system. Maybe it will spread to other companies. Someday it may be considered part of the general performance routine—and might even be named after you!

In other words, I framed his idea by making it seem that it could be successful in a realistic way. The young manager went from feeling insignificant to feeling great.

Use conversations to commit: When you're talking to someone you've known for a while, stop in the middle of a tough conversation and say, "I've always liked you, and I am committed to your success."

These are hard statements to make, because each one is a commitment that will be remembered. Each one consigns you to be true to your words because you've raised the stakes. If you think you disappoint people with apathy, try disappointing them after you've committed yourself with compassion.

So many of our conversations are mechanical. We move through a set of points we have to accomplish and then we race for the water cooler, the plane, or the TV. Instead, be a warm person: Listen, aspire, help—do all the things a machine can't do.

After my day ends I work on improving my conversational skills. Like a football coach, I run the tapes of the day's game plays in my mind. I think about missed opportunities. I think about mistakes. I think about whether I framed a conversation correctly, guided it well, made committal statements. Was I humane? Can I improve my conversation in ways that will deepen the relationship?

I've developed a new practice as an adjunct to conversations: We all shoot scads of photos on vacation, but what about at work? My wife recently gave me a digital camera and it's become part of my bizlove arsenal. After every meeting, when it feels appropriate, I have a picture taken with myself and my new target for professional affection. The photo forever retains the warm memory. Sometimes I e-mail the photo as part of my lovecat follow-up. Other times I print it out, frame or mat it, and mail it. Often people place the picture in their office next to their family pics for others to see.

Quick Opps

These are those swift junctures where we converse in short phone calls; meet in hallways, parking lots, or bathrooms; sweep past each other at the candy vending machines. All such meetings can be rewarding, no matter how brief. After all, it's obvious to everyone, especially the post office and the telephone companies, that e-mail and electronic messaging are fast replacing letters and phone calls.

You can plow right through these encounters like an automaton, but true lovecats slow down and take the chance to express themselves. Because you have such a small amount of time, you can't come on overly strong—you can't blather mindlessly about how much you care for someone while they're busy pouring hot coffee and checking their mail. But there's always the possibility for a small expression of bizlove.

Just recently I was in an online conversation with an acquaintance named Derek Nwamadi, who sent me an instant message to say that he had resigned from his job. We went back and forth for a few lines when, inspired, I sent him my number and asked him to call. I then told Derek that I looked forward to a friendship with him, that all I wanted for him was happiness, and I promised to think up some valuable advice. Here a three-minute quick opp escalated to some serious bonding.

So take those quick opps, add some spark, increase the energy level—whatever works in the situation. Good quick opps lead to more quick opps. When it is clear that even in short conversations you offer intangible value, people are more likely to add you to their loop.

By expressing your feelings, you will receive feedback—like it or not. Feedback, although sometimes unpleasant, helps you expand your lovecat aptitude as you discover which expressions work best for you at which times. Compassion is a talent cultivated by experience.

Review the feedback from all your conversations, meetings, and encounters. Think about whether you articulated your feelings well. You will see bad plays and good plays. There will be times when you may feel that you sounded like a lunatic. Other times you'll think, "That was a peak experience for me."

Also, learn to sense when you are being offered the chance to do more. In airplanes, attendants call any drinks that are added to liquor *secondary inserts.* Look for more secondary inserts in your relationships. If you grab my hand as I shake yours, that means I can grasp your hand, too. If you give me a weak hug, I can probably counter with a stronger one.

Learn to filter your feedback. Tap water becomes purified water when poured through a filter. Likewise, you need a filter between other people's raw responses to your compassion to understand what those responses truly mean.

Some people won't react the first few times. So I have a filter that says that it's okay to have no reaction. Other people may look away. I have a filter that says being uncomfortable is okay. Other people may laugh nervously—and there's a filter to deal with that, too.

Don't let negative feedback depress you. You will get bumps and bruises along the way. People who pride themselves on their game face won't give much away. And others may think you're trying to use some kind of Jedi mind trick on them to get the upper hand in negotiation. Maybe they think that love isn't the killer app—ruthless gamesmanship is. But if you are sincere, at some point most people will break down and realize it's not just about the business at hand, it's about love.

It's my firm belief that people are generally good, that they tend to love lovers, and that they would rather use the word "love" than the word "hate."

It doesn't always seem that way, however. For instance, I just had a meeting with a group of executives at a major Hollywood studio. The issue at hand was new technology. People who don't go to theaters regularly (where they see trailers) will hear about movies mostly through TV advertising. But new devices such as TiVo allow TV viewers to filter out commercials from their prerecorded programs, meaning that fewer and fewer people are being exposed to movie ads. I had compiled a great deal of research and suggested several ways the studios could use the Internet to drive business, as well as offering contacts for them to consult with. But while I was talking the advertising executive sat with folded arms and a scrunched-up face. When I was finished, she snarled, "You people think the Internet is the bee's knees, it will make you breakfast, it will tell you when you're sick. I know better." End of conversation.

I almost walked out of the room. I'm from Venus, movie executives are from Mars. My love was as rejected as a Gary Coleman jump shot defended by Michael Jordan.

Because love is not always accepted, you must deal with rejection as well as with negative feedback. We lovecats must prepare ourselves for those times when, no matter how thoughtfully and carefully we've reached out to hug, people pull away. When we tell someone how much we care, our words may fall on deaf ears. Our smile may be returned with a frown. If you're unprepared for these moments, your shock, disappointment, or exasperation may make you retreat forever from your lovecat ways.

Like it or not, rejection is certain in bizlife. People fear intimacy, and most of us have built a sense of emotional detachment into our bizlives as a barrier to it. We are taught from our beginnings in the corporate crib to set up a wall between us and the other guys. They never stop telling us to keep up our guard. "Nice guys finish last," they say. "Give 'em an inch and they'll take a mile." The old theory is that within the competitive landscape of business, intimacy is a vulnerability equated with weakness.

Therefore you may have to invade people's corporate

space to establish this intimacy. That makes love a corporate challenge. You are indeed taking a risk, but remember: This is a personal risk, which is different from the standard business risk. In other words, let's say that your job is selling widgets. You didn't invent them, you don't own a stake in them, you are simply a sales rep for them. If the product fails, it is not personal risk. It is assigned risk. You assigned that risk to yourself when you took the job. You normally don't have to put your heart on your sleeve when you represent a widget, or any product or company.

Entrepreneurs and inventors are different—they assume personal risk because of their intimate connection to their product. But most of us live in a world of assigned risk; we take on personal risk in business only when we make ourselves vulnerable with other people as human beings. When the Powerful Boss opens up and allows herself to communicate on a peer level with her employees, they may ignore her or dislike her, as well as respect her. Her risk is much more intense than a professional one would be.

Yet true calamities due to this kind of personal risk are rare; the mistakes we make being nice yield only small penalties. Yes, errors can lead to individual irritations. But being nice doesn't destroy business relations, nor financing, nor companies. If other people find a lovecat's approach too soft and mushy, they won't stop doing business with his or her company; they may just not care much for that lovecat.

On the other hand, if they spot an overtly hostile person within that company, they may well not want to do business with such a firm.

Still, outright rejection will occur. What do you do?

There is no quick fix. But don't give up. Instead, take a deep breath. Discount that initial rejection. It's common for people to ignore a lovecat's first overture. This first retreat is often a reflex action, just as we all kick when the doctor taps us on the knee. It's not the same as deep rejection, where the other person is insulted and pulls away. Place those reactions in different piles.

These first rejections diminish over time as you gain experience. Two years ago, I dealt with full-out rejection about ten percent of the time. Now the only rejection I tend to get is reflexive.

So let that first rejection slide. Not that you should automatically try again and again until you become impossibly irritating or you're hit with a harassment lawsuit. Rather, wait for the next appropriate insert point. To find it, continue to attune yourself—sense, observe. Then you will begin to understand more about the source of the rejection.

Review your timing. Did you make an overture in front of a third-party audience, creating embarrassment? Maybe your target's golfing buddies were around; it's hard for people to respond in front of a group of friends. Did you intrude on someone's personal space? Maybe you touched a person who hates being touched. What kind of permission did you obtain? Did you become overly familiar with someone who had made it clear she hasn't warmed up to anyone for years? Maybe she doesn't like hugs, but given a two-handed handshake and a smile, she might break out in a small smile.

Perhaps your words were intimidating. Timothy Leary once said that words freeze reality. The phrase "I love you" lays it right out there. For some, that can be frightening.

Still, keep in mind that no one act of compassionate expression will destroy a reputation or a relationship. If you stop long enough to notice the real impact of rejection, it is small compared with those moments of dynamic synergy when your expression puts a smile on another person's face and ignites a genuine spark.

We live by risk/reward in the bizworld. Fear of the unknown is large. The purpose of being rejected may be to allow you to notice how small that rejection truly is. When I first became expressive, rejection seemed enormous, just as it did in my personal life. But I learned that if you put yourself in rejection's line of fire, you'll see that even the bullets that hit don't draw blood. You'll soon realize that these rejections aren't so substantial after all.

In all these years I have never experienced a truly major rejection, I have never damaged my reputation, nor have I felt terrible as a result of my overtures.

This bizlove gig is not an act. I am no Machiavelli, painting a clever picture of deception or pretense for selfish ends. If you are a genuine lovecat, you show compassion for people because you like them. You tell others you are committed to their success because you truly want them to be successful. You read as many books as possible and share your knowledge because you want your contacts to be smarter, more informed, more capable. You arrange meetings between your contacts because you genuinely believe they will like each other, even if you gain nothing from the introduction.

When there is no love, there should be no expression of love. Never fake it. It's bad for the bizlove brand.

So embrace your bizmates. When you're able to be intimate in your bizlife, you can achieve greater happiness, not just in business but throughout your whole life. And, along the way, you will help your bizmates achieve the same state.

Perhaps the greatest advantage of being compassionate is that you help fulfill Milton Mayeroff's definition of love from *On Caring*—You help your bizmates grow, in both their outward success and their inner lives. As they sense your compassion, they start to develop in the most basic sense. Step back and think about how much pleasure you can take from making people more human.

Abraham Maslow, a lovecat from the world of psychology, calls this "B-Love," which he defines as "for the Being of the other person or object." In other words, we love people in order to help them grow in their own ability to love. We want them to enjoy the warmth of love and become more human. When you show compassion, you help others become more compassionate; you help them be the best they can be. So when I engage in bizlove, I'm motivated by the impact it has on others, and not just the attitude they will have about me (and whatever gain or popularity that affords me). I'm not a needy lover. I don't hug you or tell you how much I care about you because I'm lonely. I say and do those things because I want you to experience the same humanity, freedom, and joy that I do. When lovecats help others do that, our job is done.

If only we could show this kind of love all the time. Today, I'm sitting at home with my family, watching the New York Giants beat the Minnesota Vikings in the National

Football League playoffs. A minute ago we saw, on the sidelines, a battered and bruised player walk up to one of the Giants' owners, who was decked out in a dark suit and expensive tie. First the athlete shook the suit's hand, then he smiled and gave him a hug, and then he took his love farther and kissed the man on his butch cheek. Here's a new relationship between these two men, showing how easy love can be at the pinnacle of success.

Why do we have to wait for these moments? Why is it only during peak experiences that we offer the love? Why does it take a championship season to show emotion? Why not reach inside ourselves and, whenever we have an appropriate urge, tap in to that love and express it. It can make a wonderful world of difference to you and to everyone around you.

Last month I gave a speech evangelizing the wonders of business in the new century, predicting that those of us who are able to love in the workplace will prosper and flourish. I ended my words with the phrase I chant anytime someone asks me about success: "Nice, smart people succeed."

A few days later I was walking down a corridor in our New York City office when I saw a homemade sign that declared, in big, bold, black letters, "NSPS."

"What does that mean?" I asked the Yahoo! in whose cubicle the sign hung.

The guy looked at me quizzically. "Don't you remember?" he asked. "It's what you said. Nice, smart people succeed. NSPS, dude!"

It's true. They do. If you follow the steps proposed in this book, you will eventually become that silk-spinning, opportunity-making, value-baking lovecat.

But it's not necessarily easy. My road had plenty of bumps, and yours may, too. There were even a few times when I got it all wrong, just as you may.

For instance, following the Victoria's Secret show, I was beginning to realize the fruits of my lovecat ways. I was reading books continually and evangelizing them relentlessly. I was sharing my network and growing it exponentially. Then a friend of a friend came to my office, where he presented his business plan for an automobile website. An excellent concept, I thought. I passed along some ideas, talked about networking, and promised to introduce him to some money guys.

But besides being a burgeoning lovecat, I led a chaotic life back then. Yahoo! had just bought Broadcast.com and I had a gazillion balls in the air. I was too busy. My automobile-website friend would send me an e-mail and I'd forget to follow up. He would call and I'd forget to call back. There was just too much buffering going on inside my head—I didn't have enough personal bandwidth available for the guy. I hurt his feelings. He stopped trying to contact me.

Two years later, we exchanged some e-mail and he expressed his anger. "You didn't do what you said you would do," he said. "My company has done well, but that's despite your disappearing act."

He was right. I had disappeared. I blundered. As mentioned, when you break your promise to be a lovecat, people feel worse than if you had simply ignored them in the first place. And I, in turn, ended up losing my credibility with this man. He could have easily taken his complaints viral and hurt me at a time when I was building my brand. Today I am trying to make it up to him. Wish me luck.

But good lovecats learn from mistakes. When I look back on the process, I realize I'd been too busy to take on the responsibility of helping this man. I should have met with him, recommended some books, and then said, "I can't do any more now. I'm swamped." We would have had a good, honest hour together and stopped there.

What I learned was that growth has natural limits. As the lovecat system begins to kick into gear, you must be careful not to overextend yourself. I promised this man too much. Perhaps I wasn't as honest as I should have been, perhaps I overestimated what I could deliver to him. It doesn't matter, because at the end of the day it didn't work and I deserve the blame.

Other problems will arise. For example, it can be hard to become a knowledge master. It's not much fun unless you're able to find frequent outlets for your newly acquired knowledge in battle. Whenever I talk about books and I see their messages light up all the faces around me, the next book I read is as entertaining as any Harry Potter novel—even if it's a Harvard Business School treatise on global microeconomics.

But as you first start to stockpile, your reading won't be immediately applicable. You may have to go through twenty books before you get the chance to use one. It can take a while. It can seem boring. It can feel tedious.

When I was first stockpiling knowledge, I took on Philip Kotler's *Kotler on Marketing,* a seminal college textbook. Easily the hardest book I'd ever slogged through, it practically bored me to tears. I would have vastly preferred falling asleep on the airplane, or going to bed earlier, or just watching the tube.

But I knew the loving thing was to keep trying, to keep reading, to keep working, and that it would pay off. Or, at least, I hoped so.

A few weeks later I finished the book on a plane, with no idea how I would ever use its knowledge. Forty-eight hours later, I was quoting an important section to a thousand people at a marketing conference, telling them that the cost of attracting a new customer is five times the cost of keeping a current customer happy, and that customer profitability tends to grow with the length of customer tenure (longer-term customers tend to buy more, they recommend the company more, and they cost the company less). And, the cost to maintain them is lower because they don't complain as much as unhappy customers.

These insights gave me fresh perspective on what marketing is all about: retaining your customers. Until that time I had always talked about accumulating new customers through marketing.

I soon received dozens of e-mails from conference attendees thanking me for introducing them to these ideas. This happened just as I was ready to give up on Kotler. And if I had done that, I might have given up on the whole system. Sometimes life is a cliff-hanger and you're snatched from the jaws of death with only seconds to spare.

Here's still another kind of problem lovecats encounter: getting cut out of your own loop. I first met Stuart Shapiro when he was running a little start-up company called Woodstock.com. The idea was to broadcast the 1999 Woodstock festival on the Web, live and on demand. It seemed like outstanding content for Broadcast.com.

I knew that Stuart was a couple of dollars short of affording our service, so I started thinking out of the box because I liked him so much. We were already sharing books and our networks, we were already showing compassion to each other. I knew I could find a way to help.

At the time, Microsoft, focused on showcasing its new streaming media player software, was funding a pool to help others pay for companies like ours to produce high-value webcasts. So I gave Stuart direct access to Microsoft executives and then disappeared, thinking that Microsoft would help pay for the event. Next thing I knew, Broadcast.com had lost the job to a start-up streaming media company that a Microsoft connection had recommended to Stuart; they'd agreed to produce the event for almost nothing. I was left out in the cold.

This was not a popular consequence at Broadcast.com. You're not supposed to give a major event away to your competitors because you're trying to be nice. I almost decided never to take such a risk again. But when I thought it over, I realized that Stuart was just being realistic. He soon called to apologize, appealing to my sense of compassion and reminding me that his company was like an impoverished nation—it had no cash and could live only on handouts. To them, Microsoft was a benevolent savior. "Be in my shoes," he said.

Fast-forward two years: I'm passing through JFK Airport on a long trip and I see Stuart, who is now a freelance consultant. We hugged and within minutes we'd resumed our relationship to the point where next month I will introduce him to a major Hollywood studio executive. Stuart is a lovecat. I will take new chances for him.

So, yes, you will get burned from time to time. All

lovecats do. But if you can put yourself in the other person's shoes and be compassionate, you'll see that it's usually not so bad. The above was my worst story, and I recovered fast.

Here's another problem lovecats may encounter: forgetting that love has boundaries. Keith James is a friend who works at a large California research consulting firm. He is a terrifically smart young man who reads every book he can, who adds people to his network continually, who is learning to show compassion. He has been itching to try out the lovecat system for some time now. Recently he got the chance and sauntered out in his bizworld debut as a lovecat. He screwed up.

The particular lesson I had been trying to teach him was to be compassionate with smaller companies; this was just as Keith was meeting with a Fortune 500 conglomerate where he was going to make a presentation on his company's behalf. Also on the presentation agenda was a tiny research group whose owners I knew. I advised Keith to act nice. "Be complimentary," I said. "Show respect. Don't find ways to contradict them. Let them speak first so they have a chance. You don't need the airtime as much as they do. Share the stage."

It's typical in our business for a large company to hire two firms to do the same job because they can't afford not to have someone get it right. They then put the firms in the same room and let them fight it out. It's unpleasant. But the big company generally wins, often by making the smaller company go last, giving them only a few minutes to talk, making them look bad. I advised Keith to avoid that route and instead take the high road.

Keith returned from the meeting visibly upset. The other company had taken almost the entire meeting to showcase its results, preempting Keith's presentation so that he had a hard time proving he'd done any good work at all. Basically, they had taken advantage of his kindness and handed him his head.

"I was too nice and I got burned," Keith said.

I replied, "Remember what I told you last week? NSPS. You were nice, but you should also have been smart. Even though you let them go first, you could have determined that they would finish at such and such a time, or you could have compared notes." Instead Keith told me that he had just let them go ahead without any plan in mind.

Being a lovecat is not just about being nice. There's no point in playing by these rules if you're not smart, too. Because if you're not, it won't scale, and all you'll have to show for it is good intentions rather than good business relationships. To quote the movie *This Is Spinal Tap*, "There's a fine line between stupid and clever."

But we all make mistakes—I do, Keith does, and so will you. These mistakes can surprise you, but you always learn from them.

You may also be surprised by some of the hidden benefits of being a lovecat. Years ago I had heard about MP3 (or MPEG Layer Three), a new technology that lets users download music off the Internet, even at slow connection speeds. Cool, I thought, so I e-mailed the man who was running the company, Michael Robertson, the CEO and founder of MP3.com (which he'd started from scratch using his own money). At the time, Michael called it Z Corporation because, like me, he loves to end words with that crazy letter "z."

It turns out that Michael had always wanted to hook up with my former boss, Mark Cuban, as it isn't a stretch from downloadable music (which you can store on your computer) to streamed music (which is like listening to the radio). We talked, Michael gave me some advice about building a business on the Internet, including how to raise money and how to hire strategic employees, and I arranged an introduction with Mark.

We then stayed friends. I wrote articles for his website on the future of downloadable music and publicly supported him to anyone on Wall Street—and anywhere else—who would listen. Since Broadcast.com had recently engineered a successful initial public offering (IPO), I had some serious credibility and became a highly active node in Michael's early network.

I didn't expect anything in return—we were both being lovecats. But one day Michael called to say he wanted me to have some stock options in his own upcoming IPO. (I later found out that Michael had given out stock options to all of the nodes in his network, making it the largest dispersal of friends-and-family options in IPO history.) This was at a time when some IPOs were soaring from their initial stock price, and some were tanking. But I was pleased. That same week I'd had some bad business experiences, including the Woodstock.com deal. I hadn't started making real money yet and was wondering if this lovecat idea would ever fly. Maybe I was giving away too much. I just didn't know.

A few months later I was in Florida as a favor to one of my World Color lovecats, John Berger, spouting wisdom at a knowledge roundtable forum John had arranged for his favorite nodes. During a break I went up to my room and found my wife jumping on the bed for joy. Our broker had called to tell us that Michael's stock price had almost quadrupled; we sold it right there and, for the first time in my life, I had no debt.

From then on the positive reinforcement for my love-

cat ways was continuous—not just in money but in friend-
ships, ideas, warmth—in every way imaginable. I knew that I
would be a lovecat forever, crossing the country like a
techno–Johnny Appleseed, planting seeds of bizlove and
letting them blossom and bloom as they will. You never
know when the next Michael Robertson will enter your life.

✳

I'll say it one more time: Business love isn't always smooth.
Your defeats can sting, embarrass, or depress. Occasionally people may completely misunderstand you. Stockpiling knowledge requires a great deal of focus and constant
effort. Sharing your network requires growing a network
and then trusting it to others. Showing your compassion
openly at the office can leave you feeling vulnerable and, if
rejected, hurt.

But you wouldn't have gotten this far in the book if
you didn't want to give it a try, if you didn't believe that it
was possible, if you didn't sense, as I do, that love is the
killer app for the twenty-first century.

Those of you who have just started in business, three
cheers for your willingness to hear that love—not speed,
technology, shrewdness, or meanness—is the killer app.
Now you know that. You have a head start.

Those of you who have been in business for dozens
of years, who are here for your own personal renaissance,

I congratulate you. You will see over the next few weeks and months that I am merely a voice for your own inner thoughts. You've invested time in learning how love might be a killer app because something drew you to this subject matter. Some of you don't ever read self-help books, and some of you don't think you need any help. But you read this anyway. Why? Because you've probably always been a lovecat—maybe a dormant or an incidental one, but a lovecat nonetheless. All I've done is wake you up to that fact and remind you of what's in your heart. You've tried other means to succeed, but at your core you've always known, somehow, that you were on the wrong track. There's been a void in your bizlife that you've wanted to fill. I can't tell you how many people I've met who admitted that they've always felt this way, that there shouldn't be any need to go to bed every night feeling bad about work.

I didn't invent the idea of the lovecat. I am just a voice expressing what we all know to be true. I want you now to go out and be the voice of the lovecat, too. Connect with people. Find all the undecideds and bring them into the fold. There are so many—the young, the middle-aged, the seniors—who are searching for answers, who have all the necessary lovecat ingredients inside them. Wake them up. Take them from being undecided to being fully committed lovecats. The only thing better than being a lovecat is creating more lovecats.

Another excellent strategy is to take the lovecat brand wider. While writing this book I have talked to innumerable people who told me about their own particular lovecat strategies. For instance, Carl Pritzkat is cofounder of Mediapolis, a leading Manhattan-based Web engineering company. Mediapolis is a knowledge-based outfit—its foundation is neither land nor machines, but skills based on learned wisdom. Besides creating websites for large corporate entities, Carl shares Mediapolis's knowledge with organizations that his partners and staff feel compassionate toward, places that can't afford Web design but need to launch their own network and attract their own nodes: organizations such as the Gay and Lesbian Alliance Against Defamation and the Design Industries Foundation Fighting AIDS.

This is a generous and warm gesture: Share the sweet stuff from the knowledge bank, help others build the network. It doesn't scale to the moon, but it can only help everyone involved.

Or, consider the case of John Raynolds. One of the cofounders of the Navy SEALs, John rose in the corporate world to become the CEO of Ward Howell, the executive-recruitment firm. He has also spent his life committed to volunteer work, both in a professional capacity (he was also the CEO of the nonprofit wilderness organization Outward Bound) and as a hands-on volunteer himself.

Although he has recently retired, John still spends at least a third of his life working with nonprofit organizations such as Harvard's John F. Kennedy School of Government; the International Executive Service Corps, which recruits retired executives to help Third World countries build factories and create infrastructure; and the Achilles Track Club, which assists the physically challenged as they participate in marathons in various cities; every year John helps someone "run" the New York City Marathon. John has made a career-long commitment to being a lovecat, not just in his own industry, but throughout the world.

Please let me hear other expressions of your lovecat ways. Be creative and give the world some of your sweet stuff: your talent, your intangible values. I'd love to listen. Come to my website—www.timsanders.com—and share your stories.

And share your humanity, too. The Dalai Lama once said, "Live a good, honorable life. Then when you get older and think back, you'll be able to enjoy it a second time."

That's the final advantage of being a lovecat. Many years from now, when you look back on your bizlife and reflect on your actions, you will not only remember your success, happiness, and camaraderie, you will also be able to relive all those wonderful actions you took, and you will fill your heart once again with the immeasurable pleasure of bizlove.

While sitting in the back of the room at a recent training session, I saw this sign on the opposite wall: "Business education without execution is just entertainment."

Now that you've read this book, it's time for all good lovecats to execute. The key to execution is having the tools and the attitude. You have that now. You know how to smell it, you know how to taste it, you know how to scratch it, you know how to eat it. So go! Go forth and multiply the value!

P. S. I LOVE YOU

Since *Love Is the Killer App* was first published in hardcover, I've been lucky enough to hear, read, and sometimes even participate in some truly great stories. These stories, which have arrived via e-mail, snail mail, phone, fax, and in person, are enriching my life and continuing to feed my paradigm of abundance. I truly believe that you get more out of people when you love them. You produce more happiness, you find more satisfaction, and you experience more surprise and delight.

To paraphrase Dale Carnegie: You'll accomplish more in the next two months by developing a sincere interest in two people than you'll ever hope to accomplish in two years trying to get two people interested in you.

You'll also hear other stories, which are valuable not just because they're entertaining but because you will learn from them. Listening to the stories that people tell you will make you the newest lovecat in town.

LOVE CONQUERS ALL:
THE TOM WARD STORY

Tom Ward first introduced himself to me in March 2002 after he read an excerpt of my book in *Fast Company* magazine and felt compelled to write.

"We are the only company I know of that has love as one of its values," he wrote. "And I thought you would enjoy our 'Vision Quest' cards."

Each employee at Barton Protective Services (where Tom is the CEO) carries one of these laminated cards in his or her pocket every day. The card contains a series of declarations, beginning with the mission statement: Win the customer for life. Then the card lists the core values of the company: Trust, Commitment, Love, Empowerment, Thinking, and Results. Under the heading Love, it reads, "Do you care about me as a person?"

Tom was brought into Barton Protective in the mid-1990s. The company was struggling and Tom was expected to turn the ship around.

To do this, he installed a true culture of compassion and hit the road to meet the men and women who comprised his new company. The company has hundreds of local sales offices worldwide, and one of Tom's favorite activities is to travel from state to state and talk to Barton employees who have been, as he says, "caught doing something right." He meets with the employee, from mail room clerks to senior staffers, who have demonstrated innovations, cost savings, customer breakthroughs, or process improvements. Tom then asks them to take a felt-tip marker and draw him a map of how they did it on a white board.

What a leader! He wants to personally reward everyone in his company who is succeeding. And he does.

The results speak for themselves. For four years in a row *Fortune* magazine has selected Barton Protective as one of the top 100 companies to work for; it is the only security company ever selected. It has 95 percent account retention in an industry where 75 percent is considered extraordinary. It has a 64 percent employee turnover in an industry where five times that is considered normal. And the company has grown its annual revenues from $40 million to $300 million in just nine years.

There are two simple rules to learn from Tom: Keep your employees happy. Keep your customers happier. That way, you keep your company happy, too.

GIVE THEM THEIR STORY:
THE MR. MIKE STORY

Until he recently retired, my friend Mike was not just the president of Pizza Hut, he was (and still is) a genuine lovecat.

Here's what he used to do every Friday with his lunch hour: He picked up the phone and called two of his most valuable customers (MVCs) to thank them for their business. (He finds out the names of his MVCs by getting sales data from the company's customer center, which tells him who's buying a lot of pizzas.)

Awhile back he told me the story of a woman he had recently called. This MVC lived in a very poor neighborhood in South Dallas and ordered more than a dozen large pizzas every month for over a year. Mike had to call her ten times before he reached her, because nobody ever answered the phone. But when he finally got her, he said, "Hi, I'm the president of Pizza Hut."

The woman didn't believe him at first, but after he was able to convince her of his identity, he mentioned that he knew she had purchased so many pizzas. "From the bottom of my heart, I want to thank you for your business," he said. "And I'd like to know if we're taking good care of you."

"My kids love your pizza," she said. "And you guys do a wonderful job."

But because he is a compassionate man, instead of getting off the phone, he continued talking to her. "Tell me more," he said. "What is your story?" (This ultimate compassionate question should always be asked of customers, colleagues, and employees.)

"Mr. Mike," she said, "I don't have much of a life." She went on to explain that she was divorced with five children between the ages of three and eleven, and that she worked at three jobs to support them. In the morning she was a maid at a hotel, in the evening a waitress at a greasy spoon, and on the weekends she cleaned houses. Her kids were angry with her because they seldom got to see her. Still, although they lived in a bad neighborhood, she wanted them to grow up with a strong work ethic. And she didn't want her kids to see their mother accept public assistance. So she worked nonstop.

"My kids really love pizza," she said, so she let the eldest order pizza whenever the others wanted it, and that's why they had been eating so much.

Her words touched Mike's heart. "Ma'am," he said, "I want to thank you for something entirely different than being a good customer. I want to thank you for being a good mother."

He then asked her the last time anybody had told her she was a good mother. She replied that, outside of her kids, no one had ever done so. Then she began to cry. "Mr. Mike," she said, "Thank you. For the rest of my life, I will tell the story about how an important executive called me at home and told me I was a good mother."

Stories are a major currency in our lives, both professional and personal. People generally don't recognize their own stories, but if you're compassionate and observant, you can help others create them; when you do, you give them something they can treasure for the rest of their lives—a new, sympathetic perspective on who they are and why they are good people. We all have golden opportunities during our workdays to knight great people and award good souls. In the words of the great steel magnate Charles Schwab, leaders should be "hearty with their approbation and lavish with their praise."

SPREADING THE LOVE:
THE ROSETTA STORY

As you now know, love in business is a matter of sharing your knowledge, your network of relationships, and your compassion—or any combination of the three. I have learned this lesson many times in life, and I learned it again just a while back at the DFW International Airport.

After missing my flight to San Jose, I noticed that my shoes were dirty. I wandered over to a shoe-shine stand, where a young lady named Rosetta greeted me and got right to work. While polishing, she asked if I was a businessman, to which I proudly said, "Yes!" She then shared with me her desire to run a business of her own someday. She explained that she was a single parent of three kids and wanted to control her destiny as well as their future. She complained that business owners make all the money, and that she had more to offer than just a shine on shoes.

I immediately put aside my newspaper. I could relate to her aspirations. I looked her right in the eyes and saw ambition, dignity, and fire. Thinking about the knowledge I could share with her, I suggested she read Dale Carnegie's *How to Win Friends and Influence People* because I thought it would give her a good perspective on people and business. I told her about *Entrepreneur* magazine and all of the business opportunities in each issue. I also talked to her about her current business: running a household and running that stand.

"You have your own profit and loss statement, your own staff, and your own mission: to raise your kids. Basically, you're You, Inc.!"

She understood my point, smiled, and talked to me about how she makes decisions regarding spending money on education versus entertainment, and she talked about the investment value of renting versus owning her home. We agreed that everyone except the total recluse conducts business, which means that everyone is a businessperson. The only difference is that the owner of the shoe-shine stand, for example, has a different set of problems—payroll, taxes, insurance, rent—than an employee like Rosetta. So maybe, just maybe, she should study business first, and then take the plunge with eyes wide open. I could tell she was enthused and I felt great taking a few minutes to talk with her, about her.

The day before I'd left on this trip, my publisher had sent me a hundred promotional flyers for my book to hand out whenever possible. As Rosetta finished my shoes, I had a brainstorm: I would hire her to pass out some of these flyers to her customers! The flyers had the book cover, my picture, and a description of the book as well as my concept of love in business. So I gave Rosetta a big tip and asked if she'd help pass out these flyers, explaining to her that her stand was a powerful place to market a business book, since she came in contact with many important business people.

Rosetta was delighted. "I'll do you better," she said. "I know all the store managers in the airport as well as other shoe-shine stand operators. I'll give them some, too. So, please, may I have the entire stack?"

An hour later, running to my gate, I passed Rosetta's stand, where I saw her giving a flyer to one of her clients and talking up the book. She looked happier, she looked more fulfilled, her eyes were on fire!

The following week, I was running through DFW once more and noticed one of my flyers taped to a shoe-shine stand—not Rosetta's. When I ducked into a news-stand, the cashier smiled at me and, after some fumbling under the counter, produced another copy of the flyer. Actually, it was a copy of a copy—Rosetta was adding value and spreading the word. Good people were working hard for me, people whom I had never even met. The cashier wished me luck and told me that she couldn't wait to display and sell the book.

All in all, I've learned that everyone is powerful, everyone has a story to tell, and everyone is a businessperson. By sharing knowledge and compassion with Rosetta, I achieved word-of-mouth marketing in one of the most important hubs of the business world—an international airport. I learned through notions like Seth Godin's "Unleashing the Ideavirus" that people who travel can be very powerful sneezers, influencers, and gospel spreaders. I received an incredible return on investment for my time, compassion, and payment to Rosetta.

Don't let your next Rosetta slip by. She may be the bright spot in your day—your number one teammate in the business of life.

If you have stories you'd like to share with me, I'm all eyes. Send me a note at tim@timsanders.com.

THE EXPERIENCE ECONOMY by B. Joseph Pine II and James H. Gilmore, Harvard Business School Press, 1999

> Here is excellent insight into an important trend in economic value: staging experiences. The authors explain, through tales of great companies from Starbucks to Intel, why all the world is a stage—including your business and your market—and why we must use our products as props and our services as a platform to create a compelling experience. If you figure out how to "stage," you will create a differentiated, valuable brand, and will be able to extract a premium price from your customers.

CORPORATE RELIGION by Jesper Kunde, Prentice Hall, 2000

> Not for the weak of heart, this book was a gift from fellow lovecat Tom Peters, who said as he handed me the book, "Some cults are good. Read this and ask yourself if your company has the 'religion.'" Kunde says that a religion is a common belief that binds people and organizations together in common expression, and his book, which studies diverse outfits ranging from Disney to McDonald's, is a core read for people building companies and brands over many years time.

THE INNOVATOR'S DILEMMA by Clayton M. Christensen,
HarperBusiness, 2000

> I find this remarkable book useful almost every week of
> every month. It explores how companies fail because they
> listen too closely to their largest customers, which impedes
> out-of-the-box innovation and prevents companies from
> taking advantage of killer applications. Christensen offers
> examples of disruptive technologies, from hard drives to
> agricultural machinery, and shows how many business-
> people suffer by relying on their traditional—and usually
> not very innovative—customer base.

WHAT THE CEO WANTS YOU TO KNOW by Ram Charan,
Crown Business, 2001

> Ram Charan succinctly walks the reader through core busi-
> ness concepts such as "the faster the velocity, the higher the
> returns," using superb illustrations to give a clear under-
> standing of what makes business tick. This book can re-
> place ten meetings, two golf matches, and one junior
> executive apprenticeship!

SIMPLICITY by Bill Jensen, Perseus Books, 2001

> This book contains outstanding solutions that will save you
> time, personal bandwidth, and perhaps your sanity. Per-
> sonally, I swear by Jensen's "CLEAR" system for informa-
> tion exchange, which has reduced my e-mail load by more
> than 30 percent! He also outlines the power of storytelling
> in simplifying our understanding of business progress and
> vision/mission. The book is a bit chunky and contains too
> many sidebars (kind of ironic for a book on simplicity),

but Jensen delivers at least one or two valuable tools for "information reduction" that any reader can use.

THE TIPPING POINT by Malcolm Gladwell, Little Brown & Company, 2000

From cases involving an outbreak of disease in Baltimore to an upswing in the sale of Hush Puppies, Gladwell spots the sources of what he calls "social epidemics," which have the ability to start huge reactions. People interested in viral and buzz marketing, as well as market research, will learn a great deal about the psychological factors that tip the balance from obscure to ubiquitous. People love this book— I've received it as a gift four times in the last year from fellow lovecats!

THE CIRCLE OF INNOVATION by Tom Peters, Vintage, 1999

Tom's book helped me understand how to enjoy my life in business, and it became the cornerstone of my internal seminars at Yahoo!, teaching me how to create a professional service firm, work on WOW projects, and build a personal brand. These three ideas will make you more valuable and will improve your business life. This book is a bedrock for personal innovation.

THE ART OF HAPPINESS by the Dalai Lama and Howard C. Cutler, M.D., Riverhead Books, 1998

Although at first I was skeptical, this book changed how I think about the world around me, giving me an unusually cool perspective about people and my role in helping them; it showed me that we all need to find happiness and promote it in every person we meet. This is a must-read for all managers who have a conscience regarding their role in their employees' lives. Also, it's a pleasant diversion from your more hard-core business-related reading.

LOVE by Leo Buscaglia, Fawcett Books, 1996

I've never had a more intimate relationship with any book than this one. Because it's small, it looks like a one-hour read, but it can consume you for weeks, months, or even years if you wish—the more you read, the more it makes sense. *Love* is the foundation of my personal system as it relates to compassion, so if you want to know where my theories of love come from, read the real thing: Leo Buscaglia.

LEADING THE REVOLUTION by Gary Hamel, HighBridge Company, 2000

Here is an excellent complement to the first book on my list, *The Experience Economy,* because it deals with a momentous trend in economic value progression: "business concept innovation." Gary says that we can't just squeeze value out of companies with layoffs and balance sheet tricks; at some point we must innovate business models and business process. This book, with its loud and compelling voice, is a wake-up call for true business strategy!

ACKNOWLEDGMENTS

Thanks go to:

Tom Peters, for his confidence that I could, and should, write a book.

Jan Miller, for seeing potential and for taking a chance.

All of my Yahoo!s, whom I love very much for their enthusiasm and their passion.

Billye Coffman, my mom, who taught me the original cliff-and-tag system and who supported my dreams. No matter where I was or what I was doing, she always believed in me. I owe her everything for that.

Kyle Smith, my node zero who made all this possible.

All my Crownites, who accepted my ostentatious approach to their business, with special thanks to Chip Gibson, Steve Ross, Bob Mecoy, and Annik LaFarge, as well as my Randomites, Don Weisberg and Madeline Macintosh.

The hundreds of wonderful writers who have inspired and enabled me, because they wrote great, great books.

And finally, Gene Stone, my coauthor and now lifelong friend, for being my mentor, not just on the subject matter of this book but on the vocation of being a writer; for his containment of that tsunami called me; and for the preservation of my gonzo style of thinking and writing. Yeah, baby!

About the Author

TIM SANDERS, the Chief Solutions Officer at Yahoo!, consults with Fortune 500 executives and world-class brands on marketing and Internet strategy. He lives in northern California. Visit him at www.timsanders.com.